Designing Preschool Movement Programs

Stephen W. Sanders, MEd
Virginia Tech University

Human Kinetics Publishers

Library of Congress Cataloging-in-Publication Data

Sanders, Stephen W., 1952-
  Designing preschool movement programs / Stephen W. Sanders
    p.   cm.
  Includes index.
  ISBN 0-87322-362-4
  1. Movement education--United States   2. Education, Preschool-
-United States.   I. Title.
  GV452.S26 1992   92-4595
  372.86--dc20   CIP

ISBN: 0-87322-362-4

Acquisitions Editor: Linda Anne Bump, PhD
Developmental Editor: Mary E. Fowler
Assistant Editors: Laura Bofinger, Elizabeth Bridgett, Dawn Roselund, and John Wentworth
Copyeditor: Merv Hendricks
Proofreader: Christine Drews
Production Director: Ernie Noa
Typesetter: Julie Overholt
Text Design: Keith Blomberg
Text Layout: Denise Peters
Cover Design: Jack Davis
Illustrations: Keith Blomberg
Printer: Versa Press

Human Kinetics books are available at special discounts for bulk purchase for sales promotions, premiums, fund-raising, or educational use. Special editions or book excerpts can also be created to specificaton. For details, contact the Special Sales Manager at Human Kinetics.

Printed in the United States of America

10 9 8 7 6 5 4 3 2 1

Human Kinetics Publishers
Box 5076, Champaign, IL 61825-5076
1-800-747-4457

Canada Office:
Human Kinetics Publishers, Inc.
P.O. Box 2503, Windsor, ON N8Y 4S2
1-800-465-7301 (in Canada only)

Europe Office:
Human Kinetics Publishers (Europe) Ltd.
P.O. Box IW14
Leeds LS16 6TR
England
0532-781708

Australia Office:
Human Kinetics Publishers
P.O. Box 80
Kingswood 5062
South Australia

Contents

Preface

Welcome to the world of young children and movement, a journey into the specialized world of teaching physical skills to young children. It is a journey through a stimulating and purposeful environment in which we as teachers guide children to develop physical skills and to gain self-confidence. On this journey children of all sizes and shapes, of all educational and cultural backgrounds become efficient movers while learning about their bodies' movement potential.

I hope to give teachers of children ages 3 through 5 a map to follow in developing and administering a successful physical education program. This map is a simple and basic guide to developing physical skills that lay a foundation for more complex skill development and learning. Early exposure to developmentally appropriate activities helps children acquire skills and attitudes necessary for healthy and active lives.

Enter this world of young children and movement confidently, with the knowledge and experiences of a proven preschool movement curriculum. This book details a real-world example of a preschool curriculum. Its lessons and activities were taken directly from a curriculum developed over an 8-year period and used in varied environments with thousands of children, including those in day-care centers and public and private preschools.

In 1982 I began developing a preschool physical activities curriculum and later opened the Children's Movement Center in Marietta, Georgia. My curriculum was based on the skill themes approach of teaching physical activities. The Center was established to provide children between 6 months and 5 years of age an appropriate learning environment to begin developing physical skills. The result has been a successful, popular program that gives children confidence as they develop movement skills. This book shares that curriculum.

In Part I of this journey, the emphasis is on presenting a model upon which teachers can base their selection of challenging physical activities for children. I discuss the importance of movement in educating children and how early exposure to structured movement activities benefits children throughout their lives. Part I also deals with how to start a movement program in your school. This section discusses philosophy and details a curricular foundation for a preschool movement program. (*Movement program* and *physical activities program*, for our purposes, are used interchangeably.) I also include a list of equipment appropriate for young children, showing how to make or where to obtain equipment.

Part II, the activities portion of this book, contains suggestions for developmentally appropriate lessons and activities. Children can use these simple activities to begin developing movement skills such as hopping, skipping, galloping, jumping, running, jumping rope, rolling, balancing, striking with body parts, striking with paddles, kicking and punting, throwing, and catching. Movement activities in this section are illustrated to help teachers visualize how to present them. All activities can be introduced easily to young children in any learning environment.

The final part of your journey shows you how to place these activities into a meaningful, workable curriculum. Chapter 16 contains eight weeks of sample lesson plans to help teachers. Lessons are presented in 30-minute segments but can be altered depending on class situations. Lessons are presented in a sequence that helps all children develop their physical skills.

By sharing my ideas, I hope to convey the philosophy that age-appropriate movement activities are an important part of each child's preschool education. Clearly, as you use this book and begin your travels into the movement environment, you will know how to start and direct a physical activities program for preschool children. I hope this curriculum will provide fresh ideas on helping young children to develop physical skills.

Acknowledgments

I wish to acknowledge the work of Dr. George Graham and his colleagues Shirley Holt/Hale and Melissa Parker for their contributions in developing successful physical education programs. Their book, *Children Moving: A Teacher's Guide to Developing a Successful Physical Education Program* (1987), serves as a guideline for many physical education programs throughout the country. Although the book focuses mainly on elementary school children, it certainly provides a foundation for providing younger children with a high quality physical education program. *Children Moving* served as a theoretical foundation for the curriculum described in this book. In addition, I would like to thank Carol Hammett for her contribution to the rhythm routines in chapter 15.

I would also like to thank the thousands of northwest Atlanta children and their parents who participated in and supported the Children's Movement Center during the eight years of its existence. The experiences gained from those children and the insights of their parents were most valuable in developing this program of physical education for young children.

Part I

Beginning a Movement Program

Chapter 1

The Importance of Developing Physical Skills

Movement programs have many benefits. They exercise the whole body (including the mind) and not just the muscles, they create a love of movement that develops into a lifetime desire for physical fitness, and the success-oriented philosophy provides numerous opportunities for learning, participating, and enjoying.

Rae Pica

Certainly, movement is part of the very foundation of all learning. From birth, children use movement to explore and discover their new environment. As children mature they use movement to manipulate and learn about their world. We should not underestimate the importance of movement in the education of children.

Why Provide Movement Programs for Young Children?

A well-organized program of movement activities benefits young children many ways. The development of physical skills contributes to cognitive, social, and emotional development. Movement skills help children develop self-confidence and provide them with the opportunity to be physically fit and to successfully participate in recreational games and activities.

The ultimate goal of a preschool or early childhood movement program is to provide children the opportunity to develop physical skills. Motor skill acquisition is an essential goal of any physical education program (Graham, 1987). But what about children who do not become physically skilled enough to participate in daily recreational and fitness activities? The following scenarios illustrate what can and in fact frequently does happen to such unskilled individuals.

RECESS: A TIME TO SIT

During morning recess, several fourth graders sit in the shade of an oak tree at the edge of the elementary school playground. Their peers, both boys and girls, are playing at games and activities involving kicking, throwing, catching, jumping, and so on. An observant teacher who asks the inactive children why they are not playing hears "I'm too tired" and "We just don't want to play." But the truth is that the children don't have the physical skills necessary to play the simple games with the other children. Vicki's friends laugh at her when she tries to throw a ball. Jerry regularly misses the soccer ball when he attempts a kick. Lori always gets her feet tangled in the jump rope. So, Vicki, Jerry, and Lori don't play because they don't want to be embarrassed. They, like all of us, want to be successful at what they do.

TOO BUSY FOR TENNIS

Tony and Kathleen, a couple in their mid-30s, slouch lifelessly on the sofa on a beautiful, warm Saturday afternoon, halfheartedly watching an old movie they have seen several times before. But "there's nothing better to do." The phone rings, and their new neighbor, Julie, invites them out for some easy doubles tennis. The invitation is rejected: "We would love to, but we're too busy this afternoon. Maybe some other time—thanks for asking." The truth is, Tony and Kathleen would love to get out of the house, but they haven't the skills to play even a friendly game of tennis.

Such sad but true scenarios take place every day. Many children and adults simply have not acquired the physical skills they need to participate in fun recreational activities. Poest, Williams, Witt, and Atwood (1990) summarized current research findings in this statement:

> Children who score significantly below normal in the area of motor development are not likely to be included in the games of their more highly skilled playmates. They are also likely to experience problems in the area of peer relationships and self-esteem. Children who have not learned to perform isolated fundamental movement skills often experience frustration and failure when they are enrolled in sport or dance classes that require the performance of complex combinations of movement skills. Unless these children receive special help in improving their movement ability, they tend to have fewer friends, lower self-esteem, and increased health prob-

lems in later life due to their physical inactivity. As early childhood educators it is important that we prepare young children to perform fundamental movement skills at an appropriate developmental level in order that they may feel and be physically competent. (p. 5)*

Children who are helped to develop a proficiency in physical skills are more likely to use these skills not just during school years, but throughout life.

Physical Fitness

Physical fitness is the capacity of the heart, blood vessels, lungs, and muscles to function at optimum efficiency (Graham, Holt/Hale, & Parker, 1987). As we saw, the people trapped in our two scenarios did not believe they were skilled enough to participate without being embarrassed. And so they did not participate. Children who do not develop their physical skills tend to become adults who do not regularly participate in physical recreation. Their bodies don't experience the level of physical activity needed to maintain healthy hearts, lungs, and muscles. That could mean more passive, less fulfilling, and less healthy lives.

When Should Children Begin Developing Physical Skills?

Many educators and parents believe children will develop physical skills on their own. For some children this is true, but many others need to be challenged with age-appropriate activities to help them develop even the most basic skills such as throwing and catching.

Motor development experts agree that children develop fundamental motor patterns between the critical ages of 2 and 7 (Corbin, 1973; Flinchum, 1975; Wickstrom, 1977; Zaichkowsky, Zaichkowsky, & Martinek, 1980). The preschool years are ideal for introducing children to motor skills they will use throughout life. These physical skills are further developed and refined during elementary school. Development of motor skills in childhood gives children the skills needed

---

*Reprinted by permission of the publisher, National Association for the Education of Young Children, Washington, DC.

to participate in recreational activities as an adult and thus maintain a healthy level of fitness. Any preschool physical education program should lay a foundation that helps each child develop skills and become a physically educated person.

The Physically Educated Person

What is a *physically educated person*? In 1990 the National Association for Sport and Physical Education (NASPE) developed a document entitled "Physical Education Outcomes," which helps to define the term. A physically educated person is one who

- **has** learned skills necessary to perform a variety of physical activities;
- **does** participate regularly in physical activity;
- **is** physically fit;
- **knows** the implications of and the benefits from involvement in physical activities;
- **values** physical activity and its contributions to a healthful lifestyle.

Each of the five components of this definition has been expanded to identify activities and outcomes that characterize a physically educated person:

A physically educated person:

- **HAS** learned skills necessary to perform a variety of physical activities

  ...Moves using concepts of body awareness, space awareness, effort, and relationships

  ...Demonstrates competence in a variety of manipulative, locomotor, and nonlocomotor skills

  ...Demonstrates competence in combinations of manipulative, locomotor, and nonlocomotor skills performed individually and with others

  ...Demonstrates competence in many different forms of physical activity

  ...Demonstrates proficiency in a few forms of physical activity

  ...Has learned how to learn new skills

- **DOES** participate regularly in physical activity

  ...Participates in health-enhancing physical activity at least three times a week

  ...Selects and regularly participates in lifetime physical activities

- **IS** physically fit

  ...Assesses, achieves, and maintains physical fitness

  ...Designs safe, personal fitness programs in accordance with principles of training and conditioning

- **KNOWS** the benefits from involvement in physical activities

  ...Identifies the benefits, costs, and obligations associated with regular participation in physical activity

  ...Recognizes the risk and safety factors associated with regular participation in physical activity

  ...Applies concepts and principles to the development of motor skills

  ...Understands that wellness involves more than being physically fit

  ...Knows rules, strategies, and appropriate behaviors for selected physical activities

  ...Recognizes that participation in physical activity can lead to multicultural and international understanding

  ...Understands that physical activity provides the opportunity for enjoyment, self-expression, and communication

- **VALUES** physical activity and its contributions to a healthful lifestyle

  ...Appreciates the relationships with others that result from participation in physical activity

  ...Respects the role that regular physical activity plays in the pursuit of lifelong health and well-being

  ...Cherishes the feelings that result from regular participation in physical activity*

Just as educators in the areas of math and reading have defined goals for students to work toward, physical education professionals have outlined goals for physically educated persons. In preschool and early

*Reprinted by permission of the publisher, National Association for Sport & Physical Education, Reston, VA.

elementary school, teachers need to provide students with appropriate basic skills activities that help them become that physically educated person. For young children this means placing an emphasis on the "Has" portion of the physically educated person definition. That foundation helps children become physically educated and lead active, healthy lives.

Chapter 2

Leading a Preschool Movement Program

Having a plan of action is the most important step a teacher can take when setting up and directing a preschool movement program.

First, this plan should state a philosophy about children that answers the question, "What do we as teachers believe to be true about children and the way they learn in the movement classroom?" Put this philosophy in writing so teachers, administrators, and especially parents know the school's position on a movement program for children.

Second, identify goals or objectives. The list need not be long and detailed, but should outline what children are expected to accomplish during movement class. Goals and objectives are outlined for academic areas such as reading or math; why not for physical education?

Next, select a curriculum structure that serves as the foundation for all movement activities. From the many curricular frameworks available, choose one that best suits your children's developmental needs. Without structure, skill-development activities are haphazard and may not help children develop physical skills. Described in this section is the skill themes and movement concepts framework.

Next, include in your plan choosing appropriate skill-development equipment. Children will have difficulty developing physical skills unless they have equipment that fits the movement activities and that is appropriate for their size and age. I discuss equipment in detail in the next chapter and list equipment companies that offer equipment for preschool children in Appendix A. Instructions for building equipment are included in the activities section (Part II).

The final aspect of your action plan is that teachers be eager to direct children in activities that help them develop movement skills. This is the fun part of directing a program. I will discuss in detail later how to establish a learning environment and how to present appropriate movement activities to children.

Beliefs About Children

Before we can establish a philosophy and goals, we must decide what we believe about children and how they learn. It is impossible to plan an appropriate learning environment or to develop suitable activities without those conclusions. These beliefs about children are the basis upon which a learning environment is established and upon which skill-development activities are designed and presented. Teachers who are unsure about what they believe about children tend to be inconsistent in planning proper learning experiences for the children they teach.

Teachers, as individuals, may not hold common beliefs about how children learn, but if we are to develop a consistent curriculum, a consensus of beliefs is required.

Based on our knowledge of the physical, cognitive, and social development of young children we can agree on conclusions about children and movement. These beliefs help determine not only how we work with children but also what skill activities we use. These conclusions might include (but are not limited to) the following:

1. Children develop physical skills by manipulation of and movement in their environment. Children have a natural curiosity to examine and learn about their environment through movement. Based on this belief, teachers should schedule movement activities into their students' daily lives. Because children learn by moving, they should be given optimal time to move during class. No waiting in lines. No waiting for equipment. Every child moves continually. Every child has his or her own equipment.

2. Each child has unique interests and needs. Each also is a social being who becomes very interested in playing with others. Based on this belief, teachers should expect many young children to have difficulty in sharing equipment. For this reason, providing all children with their own equipment assures that all work independently at their own level and do not prevent others from learning.

3. Children enjoy structure and moving with a purpose. This belief translates into providing a structured environment in which children can best learn about their movement. Simply throwing out the equipment and saying "have a good time" does not help children develop physical skills.

4. Three-, four-, and five-year-old children have developed some control of fine motor skills but still need to control large muscles. That means most activities for preschool children need to be large muscle or gross motor activities as opposed to small muscle or fine motor tasks.

5. Children learn through manipulation and experimentation and by trial and error. Challenges to children should focus on moving and on manipulating equipment to learn. When children make errors, they should be praised for the effort and challenged to reach individual goals.

6. Young children have short attention spans, and so activities in the preschool movement class are presented for short periods of time. Children in a 30-minute class might practice 12 to 15 different activities, but as they mature they may practice fewer skills for longer periods of time.

A good movement curriculum for preschool children should include all of these beliefs about children. Teachers may have other beliefs they will want to add, and that only strengthens the curriculum.

Movement Philosophy

Let's add the knowledge we have acquired about the importance of physical skills to our beliefs about children and transform those two ingredients into a working philosophy about children and movement.

Our movement philosophy is simply an explanation of beliefs about children and how they learn that will help guide teachers in forming a foundation upon which to build the movement program. A written statement of philosophy informs parents that their children are participating in a special program designed to help them become skilled movers. When parents are informed, especially from the start, about the programs in which their children are participating, this creates an atmosphere of cooperation between schools and parents. This helps schools and day-care facilities that do not have enough money to attract parental support—both volunteer work and money donations.

Each school's teachers and administrators need to develop a movement program philosophy that works for them. Here is a sample philosophy statement:

We believe children should learn in a fun and safe environment that contributes to their developing and acquiring movement skills. Children learn through movement and should have structured opportunities to develop physical skills. We believe that when children are presented with age-appropriate movement challenges in a constructive, positive way they begin to develop physical skills that lead to a positive self-image and encourage them to lead healthy lives.

Children With Handicapping Conditions

Most teachers encounter students with some type of handicapping condition. These children have the same desire and need to develop physical skills as their nonhandicapped peers, and so each teacher needs a philosophy about how to help these children develop skills. Because the skill themes approach develops basic knowledge and skills and presents simple activities, teachers should feel comfortable presenting activities outlined here to children with special needs. However, some adjustments may be in order. For example, a child in a wheelchair cannot skip or gallop with classmates but certainly can be challenged to maneuver the wheelchair in zigzag and curved patterns while other children skip and gallop in the same patterns. Or, a visually impaired child can stand closer to a target when throwing. Children with visual, hearing, and physical impairments can all benefit from development of physical skills and should not be left out of fun learning experiences.

Program Objectives

Besides a philosophy, you need objectives for your movement program that detail what you expect children to learn or accomplish. In each lesson plan, you may have dozens of specific goals you hope children achieve (jump rope, throw a ball, or do a forward roll). Program objectives are broad to include reasonable and realistic expectations for all children.

As with your movement philosophy, program objectives should be short and simple. They are written to keep the direction of your program clear and to identify for teachers and parents what you hope to accomplish. These four sample objectives are good examples of goals that can be accomplished in a preschool movement program:

1. To provide a fun learning environment that will help children become familiar with their bodies' movement potential
2. To lay the foundation so that each

child has the opportunity to become a physically educated person
3. To help children become confident as they develop fundamental movement skills and as they become skilled movers
4. To generate enthusiasm among parents to encourage their children to practice their physical skills daily

Curriculum Structure

In my teaching experience, I have found it helpful to have a good foundation from which to plan movement activities. The foundation illustrated here is the skill themes and movement concepts framework (Graham et al., 1987). To understand and plan a physical education program for young children you will need a working knowledge of skill themes and movement concepts.

Skill themes are the actual physical movements or skills that we want children to learn and perform. Skill themes can be divided into three categories: locomotor skills, nonmanipulative skills, and manipulative skills (Table 2.1).

Table 2.1 Skill Themes

Locomotor skills	Nonmanipulative skills	Manipulative skills
Walking	Turning	Throwing
Running	Twisting	Catching and collecting
Hopping	Rolling	
Skipping	Balancing	Kicking
Galloping	Transferring weight	Punting
Sliding		Dribbling
Chasing, fleeing and dodging	Jumping and landing	Volleying
	Stretching	Striking with rackets
	Curling	Striking with long-handled implements

Note. From *Children Moving: A Teacher's Guide to Developing a Successful Physical Education Program* (p. 30) by G. Graham et al., 1987, Mountain View, CA: Mayfield Publishing Company. Copyright 1987, 1980 by Mayfield Publishing Company. The major source for this explanation of skill themes is *Physical Education: A Movement Orientation*, 2nd ed., by Sheila Stanley, 1977, New York: McGraw-Hill.

Movement concepts (Table 2.2) describe how skills are performed; they are always modifiers. For example, running is the skill. Fast, zigzag, and forward are concepts that describe running. During a lesson where the emphasis is on developing skill in running, the challenge might be "Can you run very fast in a zigzag path while moving forward?" Movement concepts are expressed in the categories of space awareness (where the body moves), effort (how the body moves), and relationships (relationship of the body to its parts, objects, individuals, and groups).

Why did I choose the skill theme and movement concept framework for preschool children? Because it helps them become skilled movers. We should not be concerned if preschool children can't play soccer or basketball. There is plenty of time to learn to play games in later years. But we do want children to develop positive attitudes and physical skills to use when they mature enough (both physically and emotionally) to

play those games. The skill theme approach focuses on developing specific physical skills through appropriate progressions. (Skill themes and movement concepts are further illustrated in Part II.)

To better understand the skill theme approach, let's compare developing movement skills with learning reading, math, and music. When children learn to read they must first learn to recognize letters, then place letters together to form words, and finally form words into sentences. In mathematics, children learn to recognize numbers before they attempt solving problems. In learning to play musical instruments, children must first learn single notes before stringing them together into a song. The same approach is taken when teaching children about movement using the skill themes approach. Individual skills are developed before games are played, and these skills are presented to children in a logical, age-appropriate progression.

Table 2.2   Movement Concepts

Space awareness (where the body moves)		Effort (how the body moves)		Relationships	
Location:	Self-space and general space	Time:	Fast/slow Sudden/sustained	Of body parts:	Round (curved), narrow, wide, twisted, symmetrical/ nonsymmetrical
Directions:	Up/down Forward/backward Right/left	Force:	Strong/light		
		Flow:	Bound/free		
Levels:	Low/middle/high			With objects and/ or people:	Over/under, on/off, near/far, in front/behind, along/through, meeting/parting, surrounding, around, alongside
Pathways:	Straight/curved Zigzag				
Extensions:	Large/small Far/near				
				With people:	Leading/following, mirroring/matching, unison/contrast, alone in a mass, solo, partners, groups, between groups

Note. From *Children Moving: A Teacher's Guide to Developing a Successful Physical Education Program* (p. 30) by G. Graham et al., 1987, Mountain View, CA: Mayfield Publishing Company. Copyright 1987, 1980 by Mayfield Publishing Company. The major source for this explanation of movement concepts is *Physical Education: A Movement Orientation*, 2nd ed., by Sheila Stanley, 1977, New York: McGraw-Hill.

For example, a child who wants to play basketball needs to know how to throw, catch, and bounce a ball while running on the basketball court. The child also needs to have skills in shooting, jumping, running backward, and chasing an opponent. These are prerequisite skills. Of course, while playing the game, children refine skills and improve their play. But playing games without possessing sufficient skills frustrates children and turns them off to physical activity.

Traditionally it was thought that children would develop skills by playing games. Physical educators have used an approach that taught specific games, gymnastics, and dance activities. But this approach left out many children who did not already possess skills necessary to play the games. By contrast, a skill themes approach allows *all* children to develop physical skills at *their own* rates and helps children discover the full range of movement possibilities. Part II of this book contains activities created for preschool children from the skill themes/movement concepts approach.

Establishing the Learning Environment

One of the most important tasks a teacher faces is establishing an environment in which all children can learn. That certainly is true in teaching movement skills. Here, a teacher must assure that the environment is both suitable for learning and safe.

To assure a safe learning environment, you must make sure children know what is expected of them. They must understand the space restrictions in which they are working, the movement patterns of other children, and their own potential for moving. Then they can move safely and confidently through their environment and develop their physical skills. Setting up the safe learning environment requires a teacher to place guidelines and limitations on children's activities.

Establishing the learning environment also requires adults to limit both the size and length of classes. Too many children crowded into a space may contribute to accidents, and a class period that is too long can cause children to get tired and develop poor attitudes abut physical activity. Preschool physical education classes should contain no more children than other classes, certainly no more than 30. Between 10 and 15 children is optimum size. The length of a physical education class often depends upon the administration's schedule. Facility availability may limit class length, but ideally classes should be between 20 and 45 minutes long. Teachers who have less than 20 minutes for class can still use this curriculum if they limit class time to one or two activities.

With some groups of children, a positive learning environment can be established in a few weeks; with others it may take much longer. Much depends on the children's experiences and flexibility in learning new procedures.

It is important to understand what a movement class for young children might look like. Let's visit a class of 4-year-olds and see how one teacher might set up a learning environment. This is also a brief look at one of the suggested lesson plans outlined in chapter 16. (When you reach that section, refer to this description if you have questions.)

OBSERVATION OF 4-YEAR-OLD CHILDREN PARTICIPATING IN THEIR FIRST MOVEMENT CLASS

Ten 4-year-old children walk quietly and apprehensively down a school hallway and enter, for the first time, a large, carpeted room. One of the first sights they see is the smiling face of Mrs. Phillips, their classroom teacher. She also is their physical education instructor. (This school cannot afford a full-time physical education teacher.) "We are really going to have fun today!" Mrs. Phillips tells the students.

Mrs. Phillips asks each child to pick a small carpet square from a pile and carry it to the center of the room. "Let's place our carpet squares in a circle and then sit on the carpets," she says. As the children sit, Mrs. Phillips observes that the shape is more a figure eight than a circle and that many children are sitting very close to each other. "Does this look like a circle?" she asks. Some children say no, others are not sure what a circle is supposed to look like. Mrs. Phillips helps arrange the carpets in a circle and then leads the children in a discussion about what a circle is, about general and self-space, and about not getting too close to friends while moving around the room. About 2 minutes have passed since the children entered the room.

Mrs. Phillips quickly explains the two rhythm sticks she holds. "These two sticks are my 'stop' signal. When I strike them together I would like you to stop, freeze your body, and not move." She demonstrates by striking the sticks together and freezing. "Can you stand up and start walking around the room and stay as far away from your friends as you can? If you see anyone getting close to you, it is your job to get away from them." The children jump up and start moving through the room. "This is fun!" David shouts. Every 15 to 20 seconds, Mrs. Phillips strikes the sticks together and all children stop moving. Mrs. Phillips asks the children if they are having fun. "Yes," they yell. Mrs. Phillips asks if they can move backward, and the children are off again. Each time Mrs. Phillips strikes the sticks, the children stop for about 5 seconds and she gives them the next challenge. "Show me you can hop on one foot." "Show me you can gallop around the room, but be careful not to get close to your friends." When the children have trouble with a challenge, Mrs. Phillips strikes the sticks together to stop the children so she can demonstrate how to do the challenge. Quickly, the children move again, walking, hopping, galloping, and running. Mrs. Phillips also guides the students in the directions, pathways, and speeds in which the movements can be performed.

After about 4 minutes, Mrs. Phillips can see the children are getting tired. She strikes the sticks together and points to three piles of beanbags. "Would you walk over without touching any of your friends and pick up a beanbag, and then place the beanbag on your head? Can you balance the beanbag on your head? Can you balance the beanbag on your shoulder? Can you balance the beanbag on your elbow?" For the next 4 minutes the children practice balancing beanbags as suggested by the teacher. They also have ideas of their own, and Mrs. Phillips praises their creative efforts.

When this activity ends, the children place the beanbags in a small box, and then Mrs. Phillips asks them to pick up large balloons from along the wall. The balloons seem to spark an interest in the children, and they begin to bounce and strike them. Mrs. Phillips lets the children play and explore for a few seconds, knowing that they are learning about a new toy and that they are distracted from listening to instructions. After a short time, she gains their attention and talks about the balloons and challenges the children to practice throwing, catching, and kicking. After about 6 minutes, Mrs.

Phillips tells the children to put away their balloons and pick up hoops.

The hoops, spaced along a wall, are easy for the children to pick up without collision. Children play with the hoops for a while without direction. Mrs. Phillips then asks them to line the hoops straight on the floor and challenges them to jump on two feet from hoop to hoop. While children are jumping, the teacher lays out small boxes, which, together with the hoops, form a circle around the room (see Figure 2.1). The children move from hoops to boxes practicing jumping and landing.

Mrs. Phillips knows jumping tires children quickly and asks that they stop and sit beside her. "Let's sit and discuss how to do a forward roll." The children are to step up on the boxes, tuck their chins to their chests, and roll forward onto a foam wedge beside each box. Some children do very well; most need help, which Mrs. Phillips gladly gives.

After practicing forward rolls for about 3 minutes, the children again appear tired. Mrs. Phillips wonders aloud, "How am I going to pick up all the equipment?" The children eagerly volunteer to help and place the equipment along the wall in its assigned spot.

The equipment stowed, Mrs. Phillips asks the children again to sit on their carpets. The children sing a song in which they touch parts of their bodies corresponding with the music. To sum up, the children talk briefly about what they did during class and how much fun it was, and Mrs. Phillips tells them they did an excellent job. The children put their carpet squares away. The class period, filled with movement activities, lasted about 30 minutes.

When the children next come to physical education, the class will be structured similarly. Mrs. Phillips has begun the process of creating and establishing a learning environment, a structure in which the children feel comfortable and safe and in which the teacher could present appropriate experiences.

This example illustrates what the environment might look like. Teachers, especially experienced teachers, will no doubt have developed their own ways of establishing this kind of environment. Those teachers know that a positive learning environment can be created even in schools without large rooms for movement classes, even outside or in small classrooms. Whatever the location of the class, children need to move safely and

Figure 2.1 Hoops and boxes challenge children's jumping and landing skills.

be presented with developmentally appropriate instruction.

Developmentally Appropriate Physical Education

In 1991 the Council on Physical Education for Children (COPEC) issued a position statement that expresses a consensus on components of developmentally appropriate physical education for children. That document, which contains valuable information for persons interested in teaching physical education to young children, is included in Appendix B. Share this statement with other teachers and especially with administrators. It provides administrators with information from which they can better understand children's physical education.

Chapter 3

Equipment

Each part of a child's education requires appropriate learning materials. For example, if children are to learn how to read and write, they might need pencils, crayons, paper, alphabet puzzles, and books. Children learning math might need counting blocks, geometric shapes, and number jigsaw puzzles.

Teachers also need appropriate materials and equipment to help children learn about physical skills. To learn how to throw, children need a ball. To develop skill in striking with a long-handled implement, children need a bat or hockey stick. Children cannot learn how to jump rope without a rope. Just as each child in writing class needs a pencil, each child in movement class needs the appropriate equipment.

Choosing Appropriate Equipment

Be careful to match equipment with the ages and skill levels of the children. For example, a baseball would definitely not be suitable for teaching a 4-year-old child to throw and catch. A full-sized football would be inappropriate for developing punting skills. Using an adult-sized golf club to teach striking skills could be disastrous. In each case, the equipment item mentioned is either too dangerous, too heavy, or the wrong size for a child trying to develop skills.

A list of appropriate preschool physical education equipment, developed over many years, is included in this chapter. The list contains items that are both safe for young children and helpful in developing their skills. Other items can and should be added, but the list can guide you in starting your program.

Equipment Costs

When confronted with starting or expanding a movement program, administrators usually ask, "How much is this going to cost?" Indeed, it could get expensive to purchase enough of the equipment listed in this chapter for each child. A preschool might spend as much as $1,500 to purchase new equipment. Some schools have that much; others may not. (Equipment companies are listed in Appendix A.)

Managing Without Money

If funds to purchase equipment are unavailable, many items could be donated or built by parents, who are usually enthusiastic and willing to provide needed supplies. Some parents want to donate money to purchase equipment; others donate their time and skills to sew beanbags or construct launch boards or balance beams. Parents like to be part of their child's education and including them in activities such as making equipment promotes good parent-teacher relationships.

Schools with tight budgets should purchase the small items first—and only items not easily homemade. Then, over a period of years they can add equipment. Directions for making many equipment items are included in Part II. For more information on constructing equipment see *Making and Using Creative Play Equipment* by Jim Stillwell (1987).

Managing Without Equipment

You can still present skill-development activities even with little equipment. One way is to work with smaller classes. Instead of a class of 20 children, which, with little equipment, would require students to take turns using equipment, limit the class to 10 children. Leave the other children with an assistant teacher to work on other activities.

Another alternative is to present activities at different stations around the room. For example, children might rotate in small groups from one station to another doing a different activity at each station. This idea is popular with teachers who do not have enough appropriate equipment.

Whenever possible, purchase or build enough equipment so that every child has his or her own. You want to provide children with a learning environment in which they can maximize the time available. Children waiting to use equipment are not developing skills. Although we cannot always provide enough equipment, we still need to remember how important it is that all children in class have the tools they need to develop skills.

Suggested Equipment

What follows is not a complete list, but this equipment will get your movement curriculum off to a good start. Included are a short description of each item, a reference to finding the equipment in the activities chapters of this book, and equipment items you will need to do every activity in this book. (Directions on how to make the equipment items are included with lesson ideas in Part II.)

Balls
(Chapters 10, 11, 12, 13, and 14)

Preschool physical education programs call for a variety of lightweight foam, rubber, and plastic balls. Foam balls are easy for children to throw, catch, and kick. Rubber playground balls 8 to 10 inches in diameter provide children more challenge and can be used to practice bouncing skills when children are ready. Small plastic balls are used to throw, catch, and strike. Old tennis balls also can be hit off a tee with a bat and can be used to play catch.

Balance Beams
(Chapters 8 and 9)

Balance beams give children a chance to practice balance skills by moving on a narrow strip of wood usually 4 to 6 inches wide and less than 30 inches off the ground. Balance beams are usually purchased from a physical education equipment company. These beams are expensive but are usually of high quality and durable. Chapter 8 includes directions for making beams.

Balance Boards
(Chapter 8)

A balance board is a fun way to help children develop balance skills by constantly placing them off balance. A balance board is a small platform raised off the ground usually with a 2-inch by 10-inch narrow base of support that children sit or stand on.

Bats
(Chapter 14)

Plastic bats are better than wooden bats to use when introducing striking skills. Plastic bats are lighter, safer, and easier for a young child to swing. Bats are usually about 28 inches long and 2 to 4 inches in diameter. Foam bats also are light and have the added advantage of a larger diameter head, giving children more chance for success.

Beanbags
(Chapters 5 and 10)

Both square and cubed beanbags are great for throwing, catching, and balancing. Square beanbags should be 5 inches by 5 inches and filled with plastic pellets. Cubed beanbags are easier to catch because they better fit a child's hands.

Carpet Squares
(Chapter 4)

Small square or rectangular carpet samples are usually thrown away when they are out of date, but most businesses gladly donate them to schools.

Cones
(Chapters 4 and 13)

Traffic cones are used as boundary markers and as tees off which children can strike balls with paddles or bats.

Foam Bowling Pins
(Chapter 10)

Unbreakable Ethafoam bowling pins 3 or 4 inches in diameter are great for targets and stacking. Two-liter plastic soda bottles are good alternatives.

Foam Crawl-Through Shapes
(Chapters 5 and 9)

These are made of 2-inch-thick unbreakable Ethafoam. Each 3-foot-by-2-foot crawl-through obstacle has a colored band and a small, matching geometric shape. These are used for body awareness skills and to help children identify colors and shapes. Large cardboard boxes are good alternatives; cut large holes in the boxes in desired geometric shapes.

Foam Hockey Sticks
(Chapter 14)

Made of Ethafoam material, these foam sticks are safer than plastic hockey sticks and are excellent for teaching the hockey or golf swing. For young children, use sticks with 24-inch handles.

Foam Stilts
(Chapter 8)

These stilts let children experience walking 8 inches off the floor while they learn dynamic balance. These stilts are durable even for adults and have a safe Ethafoam base with plastic stick.

Hoops
(Chapters 6 and 9)

Hoops usually come in 24-, 30-, and 36-inch diameters and are made from plastic. Smaller diameters are best for younger children.

Jump Ropes
(Chapter 6)

The best type of jump rope to use with young children is one 7 feet long with plastic beads along the length to add extra weight to help children swing the rope over their heads. A longer rope tends to tangle; a shorter rope is more difficult for children to get over their heads. Bulk rope cut into 7-foot lengths works almost as well as plastic beaded jump ropes.

Launch Boards
(Chapter 10)

A great way to help children catch successfully is to use a launch board. When a child steps on one end of the board, a beanbag on the opposite end flies into the air within catching distance. (Instructions for constructing a launch board are included in chapter 10.)

Paddles
(Chapter 13)

These are perfect for introducing children to striking skills. The paddle face is made of light, durable Ethafoam. Three different available lengths of plastic handles give children the opportunity to practice striking using both short- and long-handled paddles.

Mats
(Chapter 7)

Mats are expensive but essential if your program is going to introduce rolling skills to children. If your school does not have mats, it is better that rolling not be taught.

Punchball Balloons
(Chapters 10, 11, 12, 13, and 14)

These heavy rubber balloons are durable and move slowly through the air so children have a better opportunity to learn to throw, catch, and strike. Balloons should be inflated to a diameter of about 16 inches.

Records
(Chapters 5 and 15)

You'll find dozens of sources of music for use in a preschool movement program. Several are listed in Appendix A.

Ribbon Sticks
(Chapter 15)

Children use ribbon sticks to perform expressive rhythmic movements. Sticks are 18 inches long. Ribbons range from 6 to 12 feet long. Younger children need shorter ribbons.

Rhythm Sticks
(Chapter 15)

Rhythm sticks are about 5/8-inch in diameter and a foot long and are made of wood or plastic. Children strike them together during rhythm activities.

Scarves
(Chapters 10 and 15)

Scarves can be thrown, caught, and used in rhythm activities. Lightweight, silk-like scarves fall slowly when tossed—great for catching. Scarves for young children are usually 12 to 16 inches square.

Scoops
(Chapter 10)

Plastic scoops serve as extensions of children's hands and arms to help develop their catching skills. Homemade scoops can be made from plastic milk jugs.

Target Board
(Chapter 10)

This is a plywood target that children can throw at both overhand and underhand. (See chapter 10 for construction directions.) Targets can be constructed of materials other than plywood; teachers should not feel limited to using this predesigned target board.

Wedges
(Chapter 7)

Foam wedges can be purchased through most physical education supply companies or made from a block of dense foam.

Part II

Activities for Developing Movement Skills

Chapter 4

Setting Up a Movement Program: In the Beginning

Welcome to the activities section of our travel guide. This section contains 12 chapters. Each chapter begins with an introduction to and definition of a skill theme that will help you understand skills and present activities to children.

Skill Theme Travel Maps

Each activities chapter includes one or more skill theme travel maps. These maps are guides to presenting skill-development activities to children. Just as road maps help drivers plan appropriate routes to get to their destinations, the skill theme travel map arranges skill-development activities in a logical progression for children to develop physical skills (see Figure 4.1).

Using the Travel Maps

Teachers should begin with activities at the start of the travel map and follow the path of skill development. Children may spend weeks or months on some sections of a map. On other maps, children will move quickly through skill-development challenges. The teacher must observe children and decide when they are ready to move on or back up and try again.

Teachers new to teaching movement may want all children in their class to work on the same activity at the same place on the travel map. This is a great place to start, but you'll discover that children do not learn and develop skills at the same rate. Some children may burst ahead while others lag behind. After a short time of using this method

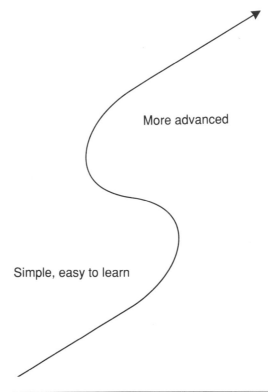

More advanced

Simple, easy to learn

Figure 4.1 Each chapter in this section includes a Skill Theme Travel Map showing a logical progression for skill development.

of presenting skills to children, teachers will be familiar enough with the system to let children work on different activities at different sections of the travel maps. This is the same concept teachers use in a reading class where children normally read different pages or even different books. All children in the movement classroom will not work at the same level. There is no magic formula to help teachers work with children who are at different levels. The key is knowing each child's skill level and knowing the travel maps well enough to challenge children to move forward or have them back up.

The skill theme travel maps are intended to be used many times because children need lots of practice to develop physical skills. Use a map for a few days or weeks, put it away, then repeat it later. Or you can use part of a map and come back later to where you left off. Do not get in a hurry and do not present activities that children are not ready for. As you will see in Part III, several maps can be used each class meeting (e.g., during a 30-minute class, students may use activities from locomotor, throwing, kicking, rolling, and rhythms maps). The more times children follow those maps, the better their chance to develop physical skills they can use throughout their lives.

These skill theme travel maps include only activities developmentally appropriate for preschool children. Children in elementary school will work on the same maps and use many of the same activities, but they may be ready for more difficult age-appropriate activities. The maps are guides to point children in a direction to help them become skilled movers.

Cues

Introductions are followed by cues—the key points children should learn about each skill (Graham et al., 1987). For example, a child learning to throw a ball needs to know to step forward on the foot opposite the throwing arm. Stepping on the opposite foot is the cue to help students learn to throw better, and it is a factor teachers can focus on to gauge how the skill is being practiced.

There may be many cues for each skill theme and many refinements that will help children improve, but only cues appropriate for preschool children are included here. Teachers should stress one cue at a time, a method found to be one of the best and least confusing ways to help children develop physical skills (Graham et al., 1987). For example, the cues for teaching preschool children to throw are to step with the opposite foot and to turn the side of the body toward the target. These two cues would be introduced one at a time during different lessons.

The more a cue is stressed the more likely the children are to improve their skills. For example, by the time a child completes your program you will have stressed stepping on the opposite foot when throwing so many times that the movement will have become automatic. Preschool children who learn cues for each skill will be more skilled movers in elementary school.

Activities

The activities in the following chapters have been selected to give teachers a foundation for helping preschool children develop physical skills. As creative teachers, you can design more activities based on the guidelines presented in this curriculum. For further ideas, see *Movement Activities for Early Childhood* (Hammett, 1992), which includes a selection of appropriate games for young children.

Many activities carry names. A short explanation about the activity is given along with the equipment necessary to perform the skills. Some chapters contain specific tasks to help get new teachers started and give them ideas on presenting skill-development challenges to children.

Establishing a Movement Environment

Space, the final frontier.

Opening from Television's *Star Trek*

For children space is the first, not final, frontier. To learn about their environment, children must initially gain knowledge about the space around them. As you'll recall from earlier mention, establishing an environment in which children can learn about movement is the first priority of anyone teaching movement skills to children. Children who understand the environment in which they are moving, the movement patterns of other children, and their own potential for moving can become skillful and safe movers.

Getting Started

Establishing an appropriate working environment may take several weeks or months depending on class size, room size, type and amount of equipment, and children's disposition. Teachers should take sufficient time to establish rules for their classrooms because otherwise the classroom could become chaotic, reducing learning opportunities. Rules are especially important for large groups of children who use equipment such as bats, balls, and jump ropes. Safety should be a major rules component. Children need to know what is expected of them and what they can expect from their teacher.

Rules

Each movement classroom is different from the next, so rules that work in one may not work in another. Here, though, are topics that should be considered when setting up guidelines:

1. Rules about how children should enter and leave the movement classroom
2. Guidelines for appropriate behavior
3. Guidelines about the noise level in the movement classroom
4. A way to signal children when to move and when to stop
5. Guidelines for getting out and putting away equipment
6. Guidelines dealing with the boundaries children are expected to stay within
7. Rules about moving safely

Rules should be as few as possible and should be stated positively. Make sure children know the rules by practicing them.

Movement Concepts

Before discussing locomotor skills let's talk about accompanying concepts. During initial locomotor challenges children are also introduced to movement concepts, which are important to a child's understanding of the movement environment.

Learning About Space

All of a child's movement takes place in space. A child must understand how to move in space safely and skillfully. Teachers all have had experiences with children who constantly bump into their desks or into other children. Many times these children are seen as clumsy or as discipline problems. Actually they may suffer from a lack of spacial knowledge and skills necessary to move skillfully through their environment.

In this curriculum, locomotor skills are presented at the same time as related movement concepts. This helps children to understand that locomotor skills are performed in conjunction with movement concepts.

To get teachers started, this chapter includes a travel map (Figure 4.2), a definition of each locomotor skill, and a script demonstrating how activities could best be presented. Activities included here work effectively in establishing a movement environment, in developing children's locomotor skills, and in developing children's knowledge of movement concepts.

Self-Space

A child who understands the concept of self-space is more aware of the movement possibilities in the space immediately surrounding the body (Graham et al., 1987). Begin each movement class by providing children small carpet squares upon which to sit in a circle (Figure 4.3). Using the carpet squares, children understand that the space on the carpet and the space immediately surrounding their bodies is theirs. Using the carpets also gives the teacher an opportunity to

Locomotor Skill Travel Map

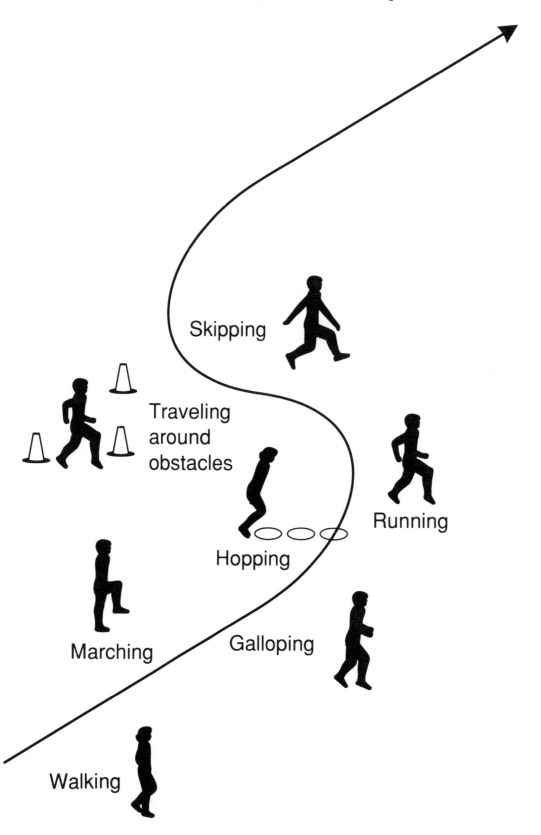

Skipping

Traveling around obstacles

Hopping

Running

Marching

Galloping

Walking

Figure 4.2

greet each child and to briefly discuss the day's fun activities.

Many younger children may not know how to form a circle, so during early classes teachers may need to place the carpets in a circle. If carpet squares are not available, use paper plates as designated self-space areas.

In the beginning, an explanation of self-space is appropriate. Teachers can say, "The space on the carpet is your space, and no one else can get in that space." The teacher can demonstrate by trying to sit on a carpet where a child is already sitting. Children quickly understand they cannot move into another child's space. This concept must be reinforced in each class by always asking children to "make sure you don't get too close to your friends when moving around the room." Developing knowledge about self-space means children will be less likely to bump into others and the learning environment will be accident free.

Figure 4.3 Sitting on carpet squares helps children identify their space in relation to their bodies.

General Space

General space is all space within a room or boundary into which children can move by traveling away from the original starting location (Graham et al., 1987). The gym, multi-purpose room, or marked-off outdoor area can serve as general space. Children should learn to move their bodies safely in general space before moving with equipment such as a jump rope or paddle (see Figure 4.4).

Before we look at movement tasks that will incorporate self-space and general space activities with learning locomotor skills, we must establish stop and go signals to help children know when to move and when to stop.

Signal

A signal (striking rhythm sticks together, striking a drum, shaking bells, or clapping hands) should be used to help children develop listening skills while they are moving. When the signal is sounded, children should freeze like a statue. The teacher then gives the next challenge, and children are on their way again, moving and learning. Children are stopped for a few seconds (3 to 10). Eventually the stop signal will no longer be needed; children will learn to stop and listen when the teacher speaks. Stop and go signals should be emphasized the first several weeks of class to help establish the environment.

Figure 4.4 Learning to move one's body safely in general space is a prerequisite to being able to move with equipment.

Directions, Pathways, and Speed

Movement concepts in Table 2.2 illustrate the space-awareness concepts of directions and pathways, and the effort concept of speed. There are many directional possibilities for body movement: up, down, sideways, forward, and backward. A pathway is an imaginary design created along the floor or through the air by the body or its parts when moving through space. Pathways are straight, curved, or zigzag (see Figure 4.5). Children can choose speeds from slow to fast. Young children seem to look at their speeds more in terms of fast or slow than in-between speeds.

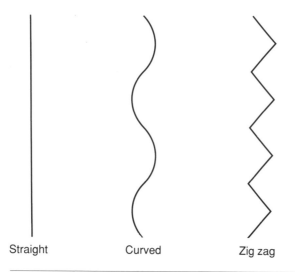

| Straight | Curved | Zig zag |

Figure 4.5   Possible pathways for movement.

To show how concepts are linked to movement skills, let's add directional concepts to the skill of walking. "Can you walk forward staying far away from your friends? Backward? Sideways?" We can also add pathway and speed concepts. "Can you walk very slow in a zigzag pathway?" or "Show me how fast you can walk backward in a straight pathway."

The idea is to help children feel comfortable moving in a large space with other children. Teachers must stress that children need to stay within their own space. As children develop moving skills, balls, paddles, or jump ropes can be introduced without hesitation because children have learned to respect others' space and can safely move without collisions.

Locomotor Skill Activities

Locomotor skills are movements of walking, running, hopping, skipping, and galloping that help children move from one place to another.

We start the space awareness and locomotor activities by asking children to walk around the room. Walking is a locomotor process of first losing balance and then recovering it while moving forward in an upright position (Graham et al., 1987); the arms and legs move in opposition. Many 3- and 4-year-old children might not demonstrate a mature walking pattern (smooth and in control) and might appear awkward.

Instruction:

"Can you walk around in our general space, staying as far away from your friends as possible? If you see someone getting close to you, it is your job to get away from that person."

Repeat the walking activity until children move without bumping into others. When you are ready for another challenge, sound your stop signal. Children stop long enough to hear the next challenge and then begin moving again.

Marching

Marching is an exaggerated walking step. The knees are raised as high as possible on each step, and the arms swing in opposition as in walking.

Instruction:

"Can you show me that you can march in a straight pathway across the room?"

Galloping

Galloping is an exaggerated slide step composed of a step and a leap. The front leg is lifted and bent, then thrust forward to support the weight. The rear foot then quickly closes to replace the supporting leg as the front leg springs forward again (Graham et al., 1987). In introducing galloping, teachers ask children to take a big step forward, keeping that foot in front of the body at all times. Children begin moving forward by stepping on the front foot and bringing the rear foot

forward. Galloping is such an easy locomotor pattern that many children may learn how by age 2. Children should be challenged to gallop forward and backward, in different pathways, and at different speeds.

Hopping

Hopping involves springing off the floor on one foot and landing on the same foot (Graham et al., 1987). Hopping is difficult for many children to master because they don't have the strength or the balance to hold one leg in the air while hopping on the other.

Instruction:

"Can you hold one leg off the floor and hop up and down on the other?"

Hopping should be practiced frequently but briefly. A good starter activity is to ask children to lean against a wall with one hand, to lift one foot into the air, and to hop on the other foot.

Skipping

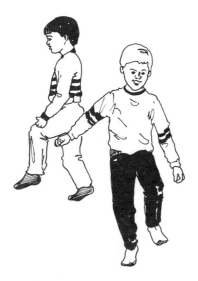

Skipping combines a hop and a step, first on one foot and then on the other (Graham et al., 1987). It is easier for young children to understand skipping if they are asked to first hop on one foot and then on the other foot. Skipping is the most difficult locomotor skill for children to develop. Skipping should be practiced regularly, but do not frustrate children by overemphasizing the skill. Many 5-year-old children will be able to skip, but others will not develop the skill until they are in elementary school. As skills develop, children should be challenged to skip in different directions, in different pathways, and at various speeds.

Running

Children love to run and need little incentive to do so. We also want children to learn how different parts of the body work when they are running. For this reason it is best to break running down into individual parts.

Instruction:

First ask children to bend their elbows, then to swing their arms when running. "The faster you swing your arms the faster you can run." Finally, ask the children to pick up their feet and move them forward as fast as possible. Always remind them to avoid bumping into classmates.

As in walking, the arms and legs should move forward and backward alternately when a child runs. Children tend to run in a large circle around the room, so teachers need to remind them to run in curved or zig-zag pathways and to watch out for others.

Walking in the Woods

When children begin to be able to move in general space and have some knowledge of pathways, directions, and speeds, they are ready for more difficult challenges. One way to extend children's locomotor and space-awareness skills is to place them in a more challenging environment. Obstacles can easily be made from Ethafoam pins (chapter 3), 2-liter soda bottles, or traffic cones. (See Figure 4.6.) If soda bottles are used, fill them one-fourth full of sand or gravel and secure the bottle cap with tape. Weighting bottles keeps them from easily tipping over.

Young children love to pretend. In this activity the children are going to take a trip into the woods.

Figure 4.6 Two-liter bottles make excellent obstacles.

Instruction:

Ask children to plant trees in a forest. Use pins or soda bottles to represent trees. "Can you plant the trees making sure they are not close to each other?" Teachers may need to move some trees farther apart. Repeat all locomotor skill activities previously practiced using the tree obstacles. This is a difficult movement challenge and is great fun. "Begin walking around every tree in the forest. Make sure to watch where you are moving, stay far away from your friends, and be careful not to knock any trees over. If you bump into a tree, please 'replant' the tree and continue moving."

Possible Challenges:

"Can you gallop in a zigzag pathway around the trees?" "Show me you can walk backward around the trees. Be careful not to knock any trees over." "Can you skip in a curved pathway around the trees without knocking any trees over?" "Show me how fast you can run zigzag around the trees."

This activity forces children to focus both on locomotor skills and on watching out for their classmates and for obstacles. This helps young children develop a sense of their place in space and helps them move safely through their environment.

Cut the Trees and Stack the Wood

Every activity using equipment must include time to put equipment away. This is important in a safe movement environment and protects children from injury. Children should be responsible for putting equipment away and thus share responsibility for a safe environment.

Cleaning up equipment, which can be drudgery, should be fun. Before trees can be put away, they must be cut down. We can incorporate into our cleanup the skill of throwing.

Instruction:

Ask children to throw beanbags at the trees to "cut the trees down." Other ways to cut the trees include kicking the trees over or knocking the trees over with an elbow, a nose, or a hip. Children find other creative ways to cut the trees. After the trees have been cut, children can be asked to "pick up the firewood and stack it in the wood box."

When the trees are put away, children are ready to start another activity.

Chapter 5

Body Awareness

Children use hands, feet, and other body parts daily in manipulating and learning about their environment. They move their bodies to be close to, far from, under, over, and sometimes on top of objects and people that make up their world. A child's life is made up of these relationships. Self-relationships include the interactions of one's body parts and their movements in turning, twisting, or making shapes. Children with body awareness—who can identify their different body parts and understand how they move and what they can do—will be better equipped to discover their own potential for movement and to safely learn about and move through their environment.

Many of the body part identification activities in this chapter could be done before locomotor skills (chapter 4) are introduced. However, to get children moving as soon as possible after they enter the movement classroom, I have presented general space, self-space, and locomotor activities first. Body awareness activities can then be presented in short segments of 1 or 2 minutes. They are excellent to end class or as filler between two more strenuous activities.

Body Part Identification Activities

One might think that all 3-, 4-, and 5-year-olds know the parts of their bodies. But this is not true for all children. Even those who can recite the names of various parts might

not understand the relationships of those parts and their potential for movement. A list of some body parts for children to identify is included in Table 5.1; add others as needed.

The Name Game

A fun beginning activity is simply to ask children to touch with their hands different parts of the body. Children can be sitting on their carpet squares in a circle at the end of class.

Instruction:

"Can you touch your head (shoulders, knees, toes, feet, and so on)?" Children seem to enjoy this game even more when it is quick. "I am going to name body parts as fast as I can; see if you can keep up with me."

Table 5.1   Identifiable Body Parts

Head	Back	Nose
Shoulders	Front	Mouth
Neck	Side	Chin
Chest	Waist	Elbow
Stomach	Arms	Wrist
Hips	Ears	Hands
Legs	Eyes	Fingers
Knees	Ankles	Feet
Toes	Back	

By age 5, most children can easily identify the different parts of their bodies.

Identification Point Game

After children develop a vocabulary of body parts, ask them to use those body parts in relation to objects in their environment.

Instruction:

"Can you point to the wall with your knee (nose, head, foot, elbow)?"

Body Part Music Activities

Dozens of songs ask children to touch or move various parts of the body to the beat of the music. (See chapter 15 for more information on rhythmic activities.) Songs such as the following make learning fun.

My Head, My Shoulders, My Knees, My Toes

This popular song has been used in children's programs for many years. Children follow the words and touch correct body parts as they go. At the words "let's all join hands together," children either join hands in a circle or clap hands together.

Lyrics

My head, my shoulders, my knees, my toes.
My head, my shoulders, my knees, my toes.
My head, my shoulders, my knees, my toes.
Let's all join hands together.*

(Repeat twice)

Tony Chestnut

Children love this song. The music is on record and cassette but can also be sung by teachers and students without accompaniment. See Appendix A for information on where to get records.

Start by telling children they have a body part friend with them all the time—Tony Chestnut. As children sing they touch each body part as it is named. The "To" in Tony stands for toe, and the children touch their toes; the "ny" in Tony stands for knee, and the children touch their knees; the "Chest"

*Copyright 1982 by Kimbo Educational Records. Used by permission.

Body Awareness Travel Map

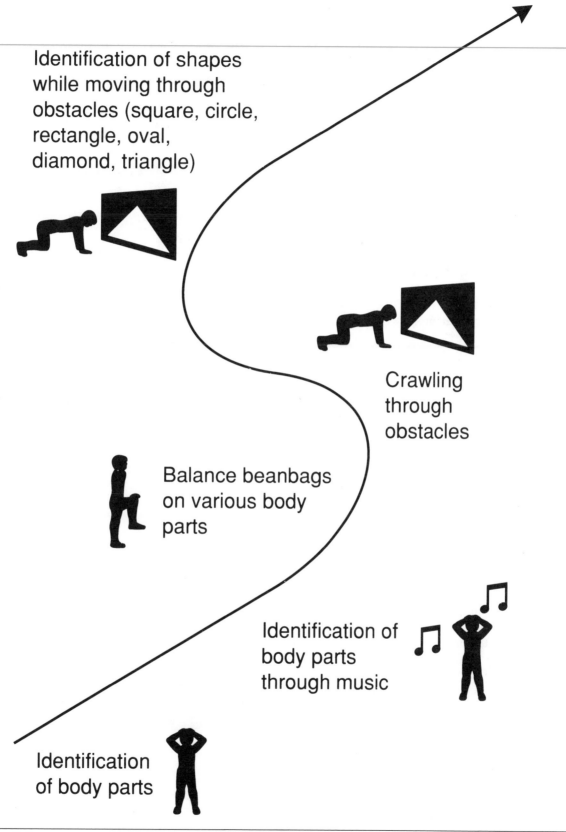

Identification of shapes while moving through obstacles (square, circle, rectangle, oval, diamond, triangle)

Crawling through obstacles

Balance beanbags on various body parts

Identification of body parts through music

Identification of body parts

Figure 5.1

in Chestnut stands for chest, and the children touch their chests; and the "nut" in Chestnut refers to the child's head, and the children touch their heads. For the word "knows," children touch their noses. For the words "love you," have each child hug himself or herself and point to the teacher or a friend. For the words "that's what," children clap hands once for each word.

Lyrics

Tony Chestnut knows I love you,
Tony knows, Tony knows.
Tony Chestnut knows I love you,
That's what Tony knows.*

(Repeat at least twice)

Beanbag Balancing

In these activities, children learn by balancing beanbags on various body parts. Square, flat beanbags work best.

Balance One

To start, children balance one beanbag.

Instruction:

Ask each child to get a beanbag and stand away from their friends. Ask the following questions and help the children respond. "Can you balance the beanbag on your head (elbow, shoulder, knee, foot, back)?" Make the task harder by asking children to move in various directions with beanbags balanced on particular body parts. "Can you walk backward with the beanbag balanced on your shoulder? Show me that you can walk on your hands and feet with the beanbag balanced on your back. Can you spin in a circle with your beanbag balanced on your elbow?"

Balance Two

As children develop skill in identifying body parts, challenge them to balance two or more beanbags on different body parts. Directional concepts and locomotor skills can also be added.

*Copyright 1985 by Kimbo Educational Records. Used by permission.

Instruction:

"Can you balance a beanbag on each shoulder while you are walking backward? Can you balance a beanbag on both a shoulder and your head while moving sideways? Can you balance a beanbag on each elbow and spin slowly in a circle? Show me you can walk on your hands and feet with two beanbags balanced on your back."

Over, Under, Around, Through

Another way to help children become aware of their bodies is to create spaces for them to move over, under, around, and through. Children find great fun in crawling through shapes and tunnels, moving over and around obstacles, and crawling under objects. Small spaces challenge children to move slowly and to control their movement.

Obstacle Course

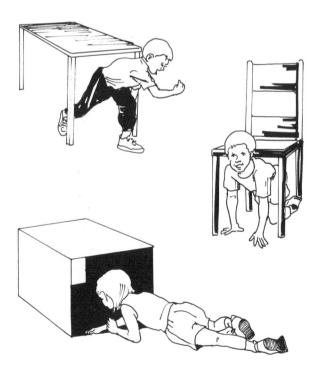

Children enjoy making choices about their movement, and an obstacle course in a movement classroom provides children those opportunities. If you do not have a lot of equipment, use chairs and desks. Construct some obstacles for children to go over, some for them to go under, and some to go through.

Instruction:

"Today we are going to work on going over, under, around, or through the obstacles in our environment. Your job is to move slowly and try not to touch any of the obstacles. When you move, I would like you to say out loud what you are doing—for example, 'under' or 'around.' "

Crawl-Through Shapes

This exercise helps children identify shapes and understand relationships between the body and the obstacles. Initially, the teacher should name the shapes the children will move through. Shapes children can identify at this age include circle, square, triangle, diamond, oval, and rectangle. As children move, they are asked to identify the shapes by naming them aloud.

Equipment:

Geometric crawl-through shapes can be purchased through most elementary physical education catalogs. Large cardboard boxes with shapes cut out of the sides work well as alternatives.

Chapter 6

Jumping and Landing

Jumping is a locomotor movement in which the body propels itself off the ground, or off an apparatus, into a brief period of flight (Graham et al., 1987) before landing. (See Figure 6.1.) Children should land on both feet with a wide enough base of support to maintain balance and not fall. Within a preschool class some children are good jumpers and others have not developed much jumping skill.

Figure 6.1 A jump propels the body into a brief period of flight.

Jumping and Landing Activities

Children can perform several jumping patterns (see Table 6.1), but in introducing jumping to young children you should emphasize jumping off two feet and landing on two feet. This jumping pattern builds success and self-confidence.

Table 6.1 Jumping and Landing Patterns

Two-foot takeoff to a one-foot landing

Two-foot takeoff to a two-foot landing

One-foot takeoff to a landing on the same foot (hop)

One-foot takeoff to a landing on the other foot (leap)

One-foot takeoff to a two-foot landing

Jumping Cues
The key points (illustrated in Figure 6.2) that young children should learn about jumping are these: 1. Takeoff: Child bends knees and crouches body ready to jump. Child swings arms forward and upward to take off from the ground.   2. Flight: Child extends arms into the air as feet leave the floor.   3. Landing: Child lands with feet apart and body over feet.

Remember to present cues one at a time. During one class, teachers will want to stress balanced landings with feet apart; another class may stress bending the knees when landing; still another class may stress the arm swing.

If children in your program can bend their knees when taking off and landing, swing or

Figure 6.2 Jumping has three phases—takeoff, flight, and landing.

extend their arms when in flight, and successfully jump and land on two feet without falling, they have a foundation on which to build other jumping skills. (See chapter 9 for how to use jumping skills in gymnastic sequences.)

Hoop Jumping

Young children need a focus when practicing jumping skills. A row of hoops lying flat on the floor in a straight line provides chil-

dren such a focus and helps them concentrate on jumping and landing. Using 6 to 10 hoops, challenge children to jump from one hoop to the next, taking off from two feet and landing on two feet. The emphasis (cue) might be for children to begin with both arms behind the body and to swing the arms forward as they jump.

The next cue might be on taking off from both feet and landing on both feet. This jumping pattern may take months or years for some children to develop. Teachers should remain patient if many children fail to master the skill immediately.

Box Jumping

Jumping and landing on two feet should also be practiced from an apparatus such as a 10-inch-high box. For many children this is easier because they have more time to get both feet ready to land at the same time. Only one child should stand on the box at a time. Ask children to place their arms behind and beside their bodies. They should swing their arms forward as they propel themselves off the box. The initial emphasis when jumping from a height is on landing on two feet without falling. It may help to place a hoop next to the box to give children a target.

Boxes can be constructed from 3/4-inch plywood (Figure 6.4). Cut carrying holes in two opposite sides of the box. The box also can be used as an equipment storage container.

Jumping Travel Map

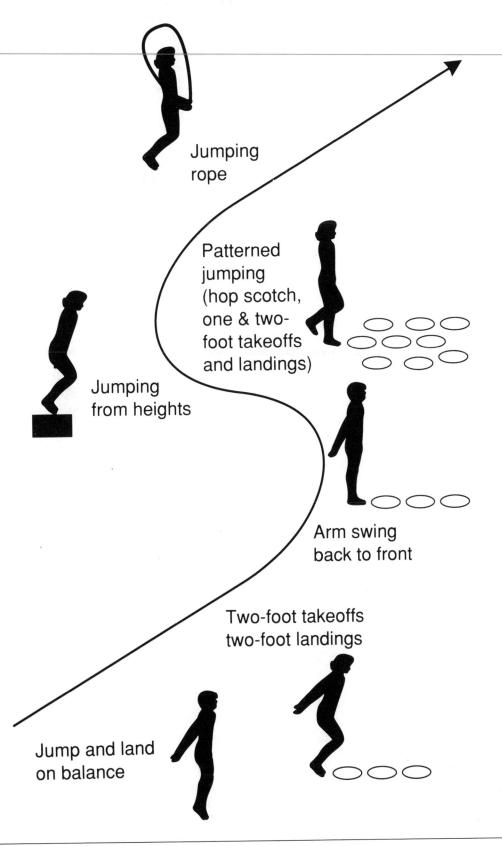

Jumping
rope

Patterned
jumping
(hop scotch,
one & two-
foot takeoffs
and landings)

Jumping
from heights

Arm swing
back to front

Two-foot takeoffs
two-foot landings

Jump and land
on balance

Figure 6.3

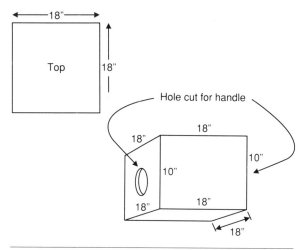

Figure 6.4   Constructing a jump box.

Line hoops on the floor in a pattern of one hoop alone, then two hoops together, then one, then two—similar to a hopscotch pattern. Children jump down the row of hoops, taking off from two feet and landing on two. With one hoop in front of the children they land with their feet together; with two hoops they land with their feet apart (one foot in each hoop).

Backward Jumping

High Jumping

After children master jumping and landing from the 10-inch box, challenge them to jump from a higher level. But take care. Preschool children should never jump from higher than 30 inches above the floor, for they do not have the physical maturity to prepare their bodies for a safe, balanced landing from greater heights. When children jump from higher than 10 inches, provide a 2-inch thick mat upon which they can land. The initial emphasis should still be on a balanced, two-foot landing. Children not ready to jump from a high level should not be forced.

Apart and Together

As children improve in jumping forward and landing balanced, they can next try jumping backward. Jumping backward is harder than forward, but the skill is basically the same: Take off in a crouch, extend in the air, and land on two feet. The difference is that the back of the body goes first instead of the front. Ask children to begin by placing their arms straight out in front of the body. Then they bend their knees and swing the arms to the rear, passing below the waist; the knees extend and the body propels itself into the air. Backward jumping can be practiced on the ground or from the 10-inch-high box. Young children are not ready to jump backward from heights above 10 inches.

Hopscotch

As the two-foot takeoff and landing pattern develops, children can be challenged with other jumping patterns. A hopscotch pattern uses hoops so children can jump and land from two feet to one foot and then back to two feet. Children who have not mastered the two-foot takeoff and landing pattern may not be ready for the hopscotch pattern. This activity challenges students who are ready to jump from a two-foot takeoff to a one-foot landing, but many children will not be ready for this activity.

Jumping Rope

Jumping rope is part of our culture. Young children love the challenge. Even children as young as 3 can learn the movement patterns involved in swinging the rope and jumping at the appropriate time. By age 5, most children can turn the rope and jump several times in a row.

A jump rope 7 feet long with plastic beads along its length is the best type for young children. The plastic beads give the rope extra weight to help children swing the rope over their heads. A longer rope tends to tangle; a shorter rope is difficult for children to get over their heads.

Instruction:

"Find a place that is far away from your friends." Children need to be taught to avoid accidentally hitting someone with the rope.

An instructional routine for introducing rope jumping is presented here:

1. Hold the rope by the handles, one in each hand. Hold the handles with your thumbs pointing down. (See Figure 6.5 for the correct and incorrect ways to hold the rope.)

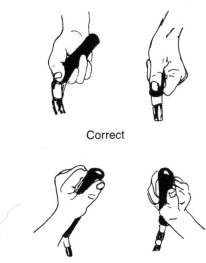

Correct

Incorrect

Figure 6.5   Teach children the correct way to hold a jump rope.

2. Hold the rope out in front of your body.
3. Step over the rope.
4. Bend your elbows up close to your ears.
5. Move the arms forward and swing the rope over your head.
6. Let the rope hit the floor.
7. Jump over the rope, taking off and landing on two feet. (See Figure 6.6 for an illustration of steps 2–7.)

Figure 6.6 The jump rope sequence.

Safety Note:

Emphasize that children should not jump while the rope is in the air. Children will sometimes do this and, losing their balance, fall forward. The rope should strike the floor in front of the child before the child jumps. Remember that children need to jump off two feet and land on two feet while staying on balance.

Chapter 7

Rolling

Children love to roll, and are going to attempt it with or without adult supervision. The young child may see older brothers or sisters rolling and want to copy them. But for most children, rolling is self-discovered, as when an infant rocks too far back and forth and rolls over. Rolling is the act of transferring weight to adjacent body parts around a central axis (Graham et al., 1987).

Rolling Activities

Three basic rolling skills—a sideways roll, a forward roll, and a backward roll—can all be introduced to children as early as age 2.

Rolling Sideways

Rolling sideways (sometimes called the pencil roll or the log roll) is the easiest to introduce and the simplest for children to learn. Rolling sideways can be practiced on a flat surface such as a carpeted floor or mat, but it is best practiced on a slanted surface such as a large wedge mat or on a grassy hillside.

Sideways Rolling Cues
1. Legs are together. 2. Arms are at side, over head, or bent at elbow and held against the chest.

Ask children to lay flat on their backs or stomachs with their arms close to their sides, above their heads, or across their chests. Children then turn from one side to the other as they move across the mat. Children may go off to the side of the mat when one part of the body turns faster than another. Usually, the child's feet and legs move faster than the upper body. When this happens ask the children to roll slower and turn their entire bodies at the same speed.

Rocking Horse

Before doing forward rolls, ask your children to rock back and forth on their backs. This

Rolling Travel Map

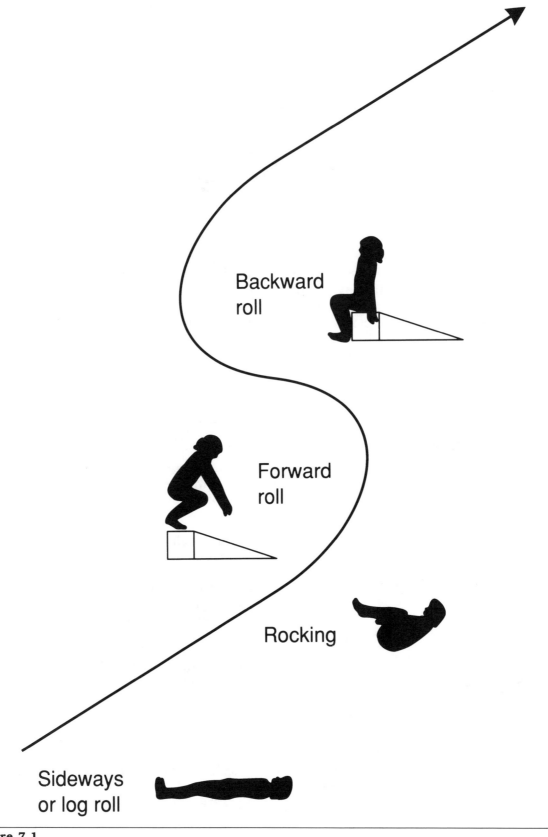

Backward roll

Forward roll

Rocking

Sideways or log roll

Figure 7.1

enables children to practice placing their body in a rounded shape.

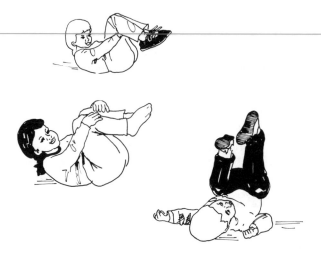

Instruction:

"Can you lie on your back and rock back and forth? Make sure you keep your back round by placing your feet and hands in the air or pulling your knees to your chest and holding on to the knees with your hands when rocking."

Once children learn to make rounded shapes with their bodies they will have an easier time doing forward rolls.

Forward Roll

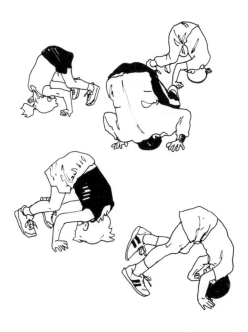

Equipment:

It is easier for young children to practice forward rolls down an incline before they try them on a flat surface. Many young children do not have the muscular strength or coordination to do a forward roll without relying on momentum and gravity. The best incline for young children would be one that goes from 10 inches at the top to 2 inches at the bottom along a 30-inch length (Figure 7.2).

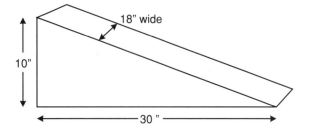

Figure 7.2 Constructing a wedge.

The wedge should be about 18 inches wide. The wedge can be made by cutting dense mattress or upholstery foam to the described dimensions. You will also need a box 10 inches high and 18 inches by 18 inches square for children to stand on. The box can be built from 3/4-inch plywood and covered with carpet. (See directions for box construction, chapter 6.)

Forward Roll Cues
1. The chin is tucked down toward the chest.
2. The child's bottom is stuck up into the air.
3. The head is placed between the knees.

Special Note:

Before trying the forward roll, children need to understand the different roles the parts of their bodies play in rolling. The teacher needs to discuss this with children before the forward roll is attempted. "What do you do with your chin when you do a forward roll? That's right, you place your chin on your chest. What do you do with your bottom when you do a forward roll? That's right, you stick it up into the air."

Instruction:

To begin the roll, the child stands on the box and faces the incline. (See Figure 7.3.) The child's hands should be placed on the mat a few inches from the feet, fingers pointing forward, knees bent slightly. Ask the child to tuck the head toward the chest, bend over with hips in the air, move the head toward the knees, push off with the feet, and fall forward onto the shoulders and back. The teacher should make sure the child's head is tucked by placing a hand on the back of the child's head and gently forcing the chin toward the chest. Use the other hand to gently push on the child's bottom to start the roll. The teacher should make sure that the child rolls onto the back and shoulders as opposed to rolling onto the head.

Children should not attempt a forward roll while kneeling because that decreases momentum and makes it harder for the child to tuck the head.

When children can do a forward roll down an incline they can next be challenged to roll on a flat surface on a mat. Children can learn to forward roll on a flat surface just as successfully as on an incline, so don't give up on practicing the skill if an incline is not available. The process is the same on a flat surface; the children just lack the momentum provided by the incline.

Figure 7.3 An incline, or wedge, helps children learn rolling skills.

Backward Roll

A backward roll is one of the most difficult movements for a preschool child, especially if tried on a mat flat on the floor. Young children do not have enough muscular

strength to lift their legs over their heads and to push off with their hands.

Equipment:

A backward roll becomes easier if a wedge mat is used to help the child roll backward. Children as young as 2 can easily do a backward roll this way.

A wedge 18 to 20 inches high, 30 inches long, and 18 inches wide works best. Placing together two wedges as were used on the forward roll gives the proper height. Also use a 10-inch high box for students to stand on to start.

Backward Roll Cues
1. Tuck the chin to the chest.
2. Bring the knees to the chest and the feet directly over the head.
3. Have a rounded back.
4. Push off with the hands.

Instruction:

Children should stand, one at a time, on the box with their backs facing the incline (see Figure 7.4). They sit down atop the wedge. As they lie down they place their hands on the mat behind their heads; their hips are now higher than their heads. The children then tuck their chins to their chests, bring their knees to their chests, and raise their feet over their heads, placing them on the floor as they push off with their hands. A roll is complete when a child is standing.

The teacher should spot the roll by placing a hand on the child's stomach. As the child raises the feet over the head, the teacher lifts up on the stomach to take some of the child's weight off the head and neck.

Children will quickly be ready to practice the backward roll by themselves. Ask children to look at their stomachs (not backward) when attempting backward rolls. As long as children tuck their chins to their chests when they bring their feet over their heads, the movement is safe. Injury could occur if the chin is not tucked. Young children can quickly learn to do the backward roll using the incline. It will take more time for them to develop the muscular strength and coordination to do backward rolls on a flat surface.

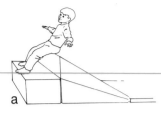

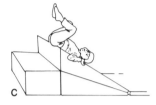

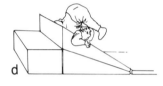

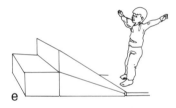

Figure 7.4 Backward roll sequence.

Safety Note

Teachers who are not secure in their ability to spot both the forward and backward rolls should not teach those activities. Concentrate your efforts on log rolls, rocking, and other skills. Children who need a lot of spotting to perform forward and backward rolls may not be ready to perform those rolls.

Organizational Note

Many schools lack enough equipment, teachers, and aides to allow all children to practice rolls at the same time. For these reasons, rolling might best be taught at skill-development stations around the movement classroom. Children rotate from one station to another, work on activities that need no spotting and little direction, and still are constantly on task. One station would be rolling, and the teacher would remain there to help children who need assistance. Figure 7.5 shows how a movement classroom might be set up using this approach.

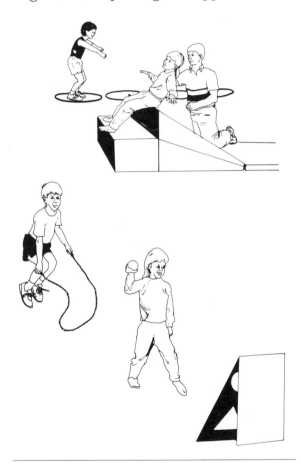

Figure 7.5 Setting up a movement classroom.

Chapter 8

Balancing

Being on balance means having an even distribution of weight on each side of a vertical axis. The center of gravity is over the base of support (Graham et al., 1987). For young children, being on balance simply means not falling over.

Balance can be either static or dynamic. *Static balance* refers to maintaining a desired shape in a stationary position, balancing on three body parts (two elbows and one knee) for example. *Dynamic balance* means being on balance while moving, such as while jumping, throwing, or skipping. For the preschool child, dynamic balance is critical to developing physical skills. A child who always falls down when throwing or catching a ball or who cannot maintain balance when landing after a jump will find it difficult to develop movement skills and may be unable to move safely through the environment.

Balance Cues
1. Use a wide base of support (static).
2. Extend arms to the side (dynamic).

Balancing Activities

Young children should first learn about weight-bearing and stillness by balancing on different body parts as both wide and narrow bases of support. Eventually children can balance on equipment.

Body Part Balance

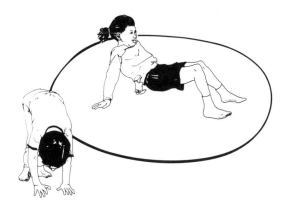

A good initial balancing activity is to challenge children to balance using both many body parts and a wide base of support and few body parts and a narrow base of support. Hoops or carpet squares can be used as boundaries for children to balance within.

Instruction:

Ask children to lay their hoops flat on the floor (away from classmates for safety). The hoops help to direct a child's attention to a particular area inside the hoop. Many children will be able to better concentrate on the movement challenge when the task is confined to a small space.

Start with activities that involve balancing on many body parts and wide bases of support and progress to balancing on a few body parts on narrow bases of support.

Balance Travel Map

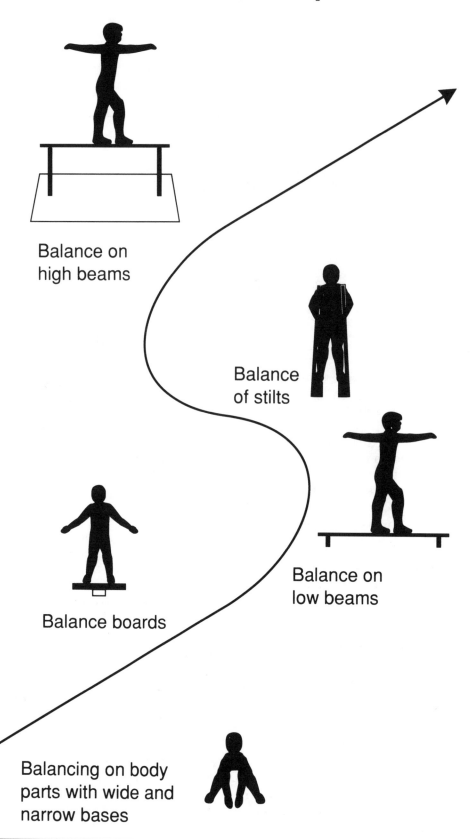

Balance on
high beams

Balance
of stilts

Balance on
low beams

Balance boards

Balancing on body
parts with wide and
narrow bases

Figure 8.1

Examples of Wide Bases, Many Body Parts:

"Can you balance on your hands and your feet?"

"Can you balance on two hands, two feet, and two knees?"

"Show me that you can balance on your head, hands, and feet."

"Can you balance on your knees and elbows?"

"Can you balance on your knees and one elbow?"

Examples of Narrow Bases, Few Body Parts:

"Show me that you can balance on your head and feet."

"Can you balance on one foot and one hand?"

"Can you balance on one knee and one elbow?"

"Can you balance on your head and one foot?"

"Can you balance on one knee and one hand?"

"Show me that you can balance on your bottom. Try not to let any other part of your body touch the floor."

From these examples teachers can design other challenges to help children develop balancing skills. And don't hesitate to ask children for their ideas of balancing challenges.

Headstand

Many teachers ask, "When do I teach children to do a headstand?" Doing a headstand is relatively safe for children who possess the muscle strength and static balance skills to perform the task. But most 3-, 4-, and 5-year-olds don't have enough strength and balance to perform a headstand. Another concern is that most schools lack enough mats to allow children to safely practice headstands. For these reasons, I include no instructions on how to do a headstand, which is more appropriately introduced in second, third, or fourth grade.

Balance Boards

Balance boards are a fun way to practice and develop static balancing skill. Children are placed in off-balance positions and then given time to distribute their weight over the middle axis of the board and to achieve balance. Balance boards are designed to be difficult but not frustrating.

Balance Board Cue
"Distribute your weight equally by holding your arms straight out to the side." (See Figure 8.2.)

Balance boards can be made from 1/2-inch thick plywood (see Figure 8.3) cut 10 inches wide and 15 inches long. On the bottom, attach an 8-inch-long section of either two-by-

Figure 8.2   Giving the proper cue helps children learn balancing skills.

two, two-by-three, or two-by-four lumber to the center of the board. Use screws (from top) and glue to attach. Birch plywood is most durable.

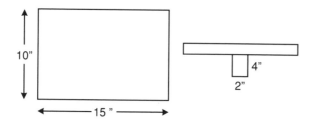

Figure 8.3   Constructing a balance board.

A board with a 4-inch-high center piece can be used with advanced children, the 2- and 3-inch-high boards for less skilled. Boards should be smooth and painted a bright color.

Children should place their boards so they don't bump into others if they lose their balance. The boards are fun for children to use in physical education class but may get even more use when they go to the playground.

Stand and Balance

This exercise teaches children to stand with feet spread apart and to bring the board to a level position. Initially, some children may place their feet too close together, and teachers will need to instruct children to place their feet farther apart for a wider base of support.

Instruction:

"Can you stand on the board and balance, trying not to let the sides of the board touch the floor? It will be helpful if you hold your arms out like airplane wings [this is the cue for this activity] to help you stay on balance."

Tummy Balance

Children are taught to balance while lying with their stomachs on balance boards.

Instruction:

"Can you lie on your stomach and balance on the board? Try not to let your feet, knees, or hands touch the floor. Can you hold your arms out like airplane wings [cue]?"

Sit and Balance

Most children can sit on the board and balance without moving, and some might hold their legs straight out in front of their bodies. But most will find it easier to cross their legs and sit.

Instruction:

"Let's see if we can sit on the board and balance."

| Knee Balance |

Children place their knees apart and hold their arms out like airplane wings (cue).

Instruction:

"Can you balance on your knees on the board? Be careful not to let your toes touch the floor."

| Mountain Climb |

This exercise challenges children to balance while slowly seesawing the board. Children

transfer their weight from foot to foot as they tip the board. Many children find this difficult; the teacher may want to hold the hands of those children.

Instruction:

"Lay the board on the floor with one end up in the air and with the other end on the floor. Place one foot on the bottom of the board and the other foot on top. Push down with the top foot so the board rocks down."

Walking on Stilts

Using stilts is a fun way to walk and balance off the floor. Stilts that are safe for preschool children are made of Ethafoam and raise the child about 8 inches off the floor. This gives the child the opportunity to safely step down when losing balance.

| Sky Walk |

Most children will have difficulty learning to walk on stilts. Instruct them to keep the sticks close together, to place their feet to the inside of the sticks, and to hold the sticks with the thumbs pointing up. Initially, children who can simply stand on the bases of the stilts without losing balance have accomplished a great deal.

To avoid falling, children should step off the stilts when they lose their balance. Three-year-old children may be able only to stand in place and balance on the stilts, but by the time they are 5 most can cross a room on stilts. Children can practice walking forward, backward, and sideways. Advanced children can turn in circles and walk around obstacles while maintaining balance.

Balance Beams

Children love to walk on balance beams, and they are going to try it with or without adult help. Parents know that a simple walk down the street with their child may turn into an Olympic challenge as the child balances on street curbs and brick walls.

Introduce children to walking on balance beams placed only slightly above floor level. Children should gain skill and confidence before moving to higher beams.

Balance beams are usually purchased from a physical education supply company. These balance beams are expensive, but they are usually of high quality and durable. Teachers need to use balance beams that do not tip over or move while children are walking on them.

Keeping these safety concerns in mind, balance beams can also be made (Figure 8.4). A four-by-four that is 6 to 8 feet long makes an excellent balance beam. Sand the beam to remove rough spots or splinters. Place a base on each end to raise the beam an additional 2 inches above the ground.

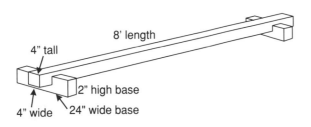

Figure 8.4 Constructing a balance beam.

This base stabilizes the beam while children balance on it. You now have a beam that raises the child's feet about 6 inches off the ground, a height from which a child can easily jump or step without injury.

Walking on a Beam

The first experience on the beam should be low to the floor so the child can develop confidence and not be frightened of heights.

Instruction:

Ask children to step up onto one end of the beam and walk across it just as they would walk across the room. "Step with one foot and then step with the other foot [cue]." At first, children may have trouble because they slide their feet across the beam rather than pick up their feet.

Teachers may need to hold a child's hand to impart confidence. Stand beside the child while holding his or her hand. Standing in front or behind the child may throw him or her off balance.

It helps children balance while walking across the beam to hold their arms straight out at their sides (this is your cue for this activity). "What do you do with your arms when you walk on the beam? That's correct, you hold your arms out like airplane wings."

Jumping off a Beam

For safety, children should understand that the best way to get down from a beam is to jump and land on the floor on two feet. Even if the beam is only a few inches off the floor it is still better for children to jump off the beam rather than step off. Then, when beams are at higher levels, children will feel comfortable jumping off, lessening the possibility of injury. Children should be able to walk across a low beam and jump off when they lose their balance before trying a higher beam. This may take several weeks (or with some children several months) to accomplish.

Walking Sideways

Walking sideways on a beam may be easier for many children than walking forward.

Instruction:

Ask children to stand on one end of the beam with their arms straight out to their sides. "Pick up one foot and step sideways, then pick up the other foot and move it toward the first [cue]. Move your feet apart, together, apart, together." This is called a slide step.

To help a child having difficulty walking sideways, stand facing the child and hold both the child's hands, one out to each side. Gently pull the child's hand in the direction you want the child to step. As the child feels comfortable and confident on the beam, he or she will release the teacher's hand and walk unassisted.

Remind children that if they feel they are going to fall they should jump off the beam and land on two feet.

Walking Backward

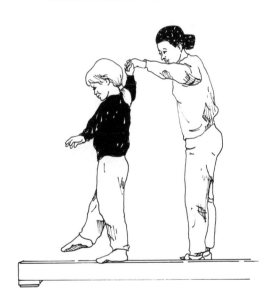

Walking backward on a beam is hard for most children and many preschoolers can do it only with adult assistance.

Many children will fear falling as they walk backward. To counter that fear, they should be allowed to slide their feet backward on the beam, but as they progress they should be encouraged to step instead.

Teach children this skill by asking them to stand backward at one end of the beam. Face the child and hold both of his or her hands out to the side. Gently push backward as the child steps backward. Because this is such a difficult skill for young children, you may want to use a wider balance beam or a bench.

Balancing on a High Beam

Children eventually will be ready to walk on a higher beam. A beam no higher than 30 inches is appropriate for children younger than 6. When using a beam higher than 1 foot from the floor, place mats under the beam to ensure soft landings. Match balance beam levels with children's comfort levels— that is, levels at which children feel comfortable walking unassisted. The idea is to prevent children from getting overconfident and trying maneuvers prematurely.

When introducing walking on a high beam, use a spotter. As children develop their balancing skills and are able to jump off the beam and land on two feet when losing balance, the teacher will no longer need to hold the children's hands. Encourage children to walk forward, backward, and sideways on the higher beam and follow all spotting techniques used on low beams.

Another challenge is to have children walk beams placed at angles to the floor. Make sure you have enough mats around the beams for safety.

Chapter 9

Developing a Movement Sequence

A movement sequence, or obstacle course, is an excellent way for children to practice and review the locomotor, rolling, and balance skills discussed in earlier chapters. An obstacle course is a series of individual activities in a sequence that requires children to move from one task to the next in a predesigned order. An obstacle course helps children practice skills, learn a sequence of movements, and learn to follow directions.

The Obstacle Course

There are other advantages to an obstacle course: Children don't have to wait in line for a turn to move, and you are freed to move around the room to work with children who need individual attention. Children seem to like the chance to practice skills at their own rates and to work independent of other children. The movement sequence is normally presented during the last half of each class to help close the day's activities.

Locomotor, Rolling, and Balancing Roundup

Your movement sequence can be started at the beginning of the school year and a new skill added each week. The course can be

Sequence Travel Map

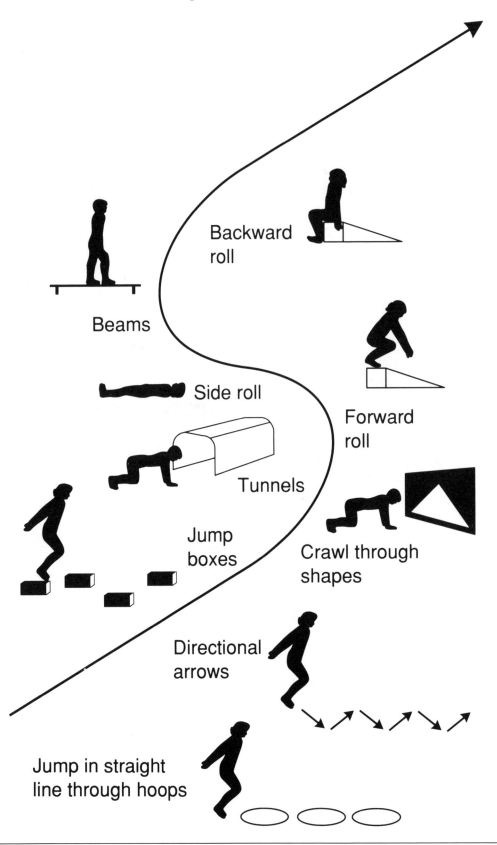

Figure 9.1

laid out in any pattern once children understand the concept of moving from one station to the next. You can use any skill in the sequence, but the obstacle course concept lends itself best to the skills involved in locomotion, rolling, and balancing.

In the beginning, place arrows on the floor to help children remember where to go next. Explain that the arrow shows the direction in which children are to move after completing an activity. Before long the arrows won't be needed.

The obstacle course can begin during your introduction of jumping skills. Put hoops on the floor in a straight line so that children can jump from one to the next (see Figure 9.2). Each week add a new skill to the sequence. Jumping off a box, forward rolls, backward rolls, log rolls, walking on a balance beam, crawling through a tunnel, zigzagging around cones, and many other tasks can make the course more challenging.

Don't be alarmed if children do not follow the proper sequence the first several times they go through the course. Simply redirect them and they will soon get the idea. Do make sure your children understand the concept of moving through the sequence before adding too many challenges. By the middle of the school year the sequence might include as many as 12 to 15 tasks. Once children understand the sequence concept, try letting them develop their own obstacle course. They enjoy laying out equipment and deciding what skills to include.

Remember that these activities are designed to help children to develop basic skills and to establish a movement skills

foundation they can add to throughout elementary school. Balancing and rolling will give children a good foundation upon which to improve motor skills as they mature.

Figure 9.2 A jumping obstacle course.

Chapter 10

Throwing and Catching

Physical educators agree that children should develop throwing and catching skills at an early age if they are to become skilled athletes. Most children will not become athletes, of course, but can enjoy playing games and reap related social and fitness benefits if they can throw and catch.

Throwing and catching go together like shoes and socks and are usually taught simultaneously. However, throwing skills are generally introduced before catching skills because before one can catch another must throw. Throwing and catching activities should be practiced to help children advance their skills.

Suggested Equipment

What equipment should be available for children to throw? Punchballs, lightweight plastic balls about the size of softballs, and beanbags best fit the small, growing hands of preschool children. Plastic balls can be purchased at toy stores or through physical education supply companies (Appendix A). Schools can save money by making their own beanbags (Figure 10.1). A flat, square beanbag can be made by cutting material into two 4-inch squares, sewing the squares together, and stuffing the bags with plastic pellets (which can be obtained from companies that make plastic materials). Beans should not be placed in the bags; they can sprout and also come to smell bad.

A cubed beanbag just fits a young child's hands. The cubed beanbag can be made by cutting material in 2-inch-by-6-inch rectangles and sewing the material together to form a cube (see Figure 10.2). Fill the bag with plastic pellets and sew the end closed. Bright colors are suggested for beanbags.

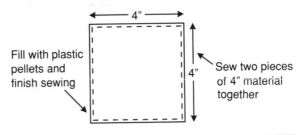

Figure 10.1 Constructing a square beanbag.

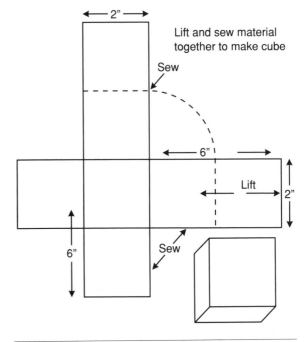

Figure 10.2 Constructing a cubed beanbag.

Throwing Travel Map

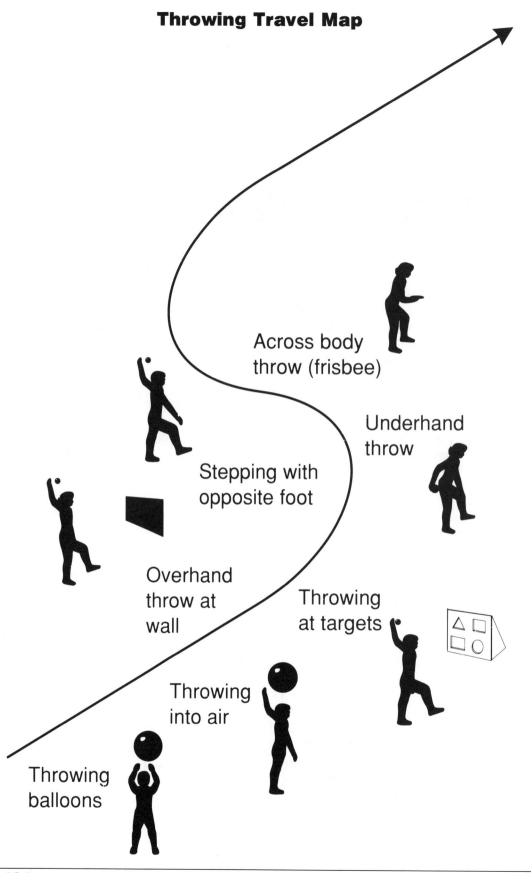

Across body
throw (frisbee)

Underhand
throw

Stepping with
opposite foot

Overhand
throw at
wall

Throwing
at targets

Throwing
into air

Throwing
balloons

Figure 10.3

Throwing

Throwing is a basic movement pattern that propels an object away from the body. Although the style of throwing (underhand, overhand) and the purpose of the throw may vary, the pattern remains the same. The thrower grasps the object with one or both hands, prepares the body and builds throwing momentum, propels the object away from the body, and follows through while maintaining body balance (Graham et al., 1987).

Throwing Cues
Several throwing cues can help children improve their skills, but for young children the most important is "stepping with the opposite foot." Children will have a good foundation from which to refine skills if they step with the foot opposite their throwing arm. Each time throwing is practiced, children should concentrate on stepping with the opposite foot. If, at the end of the school year, all children are stepping with the opposite foot they will be well on their way to becoming efficient throwers. (See Figure 10.4.)

Figure 10.4 Cues can help children learn throwing skills.

Throwing Activities

Because children initially find it easier to throw and catch a large ball, a punchball balloon is excellent for young children. The lightweight, easy-to-throw balloons move slowly through the air giving children the time to track them and prepare their bodies for a catch.

It will be hard for children to catch the balloon if they can't throw it straight up into the air (Figure 10.5). These simple directions help:

Figure 10.5 Children will have more success catching if they learn basic throwing skills.

- Hold the balloon out in front of you with one hand on each side of the balloon.
- Lower the balloon below your waist so that the balloon almost touches your knees.
- Raise both hands into the air and let go of the balloon as it passes your nose.

Timing the release is important. If the balloon is released too soon it may travel far out in front of the child where it is hard to catch. If the balloon is released too late it will travel behind the child and be almost impossible to catch. At first, encourage children to throw the balloon only a few feet into the air. As their skills develop children will learn to toss the balloon higher.

Possible directions from the teacher:

1. Throw the balloon straight into the air.
2. Watch the balloon as it moves through the air.
3. After you throw the balloon, get your body and your arms ready to catch.

A progression of throwing and catching activities using the balloons might include these instructions:

1. Drop the balloon, let it bounce, and then catch it.
2. Throw the balloon into the air and catch it.
3. See how high you can throw the balloon and still catch it.
4. Throw the balloon into the air and see how many times you can clap your hands before you catch it.
5. Throw the balloon against a wall and catch it.
6. Throw the ball into the air, then sit down and catch it.

Drop and Catch

As students develop skills in dropping and catching balloons, balls can be introduced. Using a 10-inch rubber playground ball may be more challenging than a balloon.

*   Drop the ball and catch it.
*   Bounce the ball hard and catch it.

Throw at the Sky

This exercise asks children to throw a beanbag into the air with one hand. "Don't worry about catching the beanbag; just see how high you can throw it," the teacher says.

Wall Throw

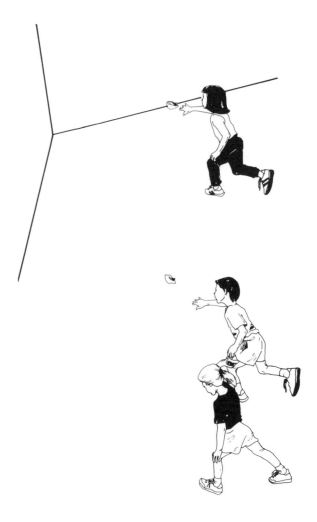

With young children it is important to introduce throwing activities that are both fun and give them opportunities for success. Research tells us that children need to be successful about 80% of the time to stay on task, to avoid frustration, and to have the greatest opportunity to develop skills. Children who consistently miss the target when they throw may, because they are frustrated, not practice and may fail to develop throwing skill.

Simply asking children to throw at a wall is a great, success-oriented warm-up activity for beginners. This gives children the chance to succeed in throwing at and hitting a target. The activity also lets the teacher observe each child's throwing skills.

Beanbags are best for this activity and several that follow because they do not roll away.

Instruction:

Ask children to pick up beanbags and place them in the hand they are going to use to throw. "Grasp the beanbag so it does not fall out of your hand, bend your elbow up and hold the beanbag behind your head, step forward with the opposite foot, and release the beanbag toward the wall."

Remember to stress the cue "step forward with the opposite foot." The throwing abilities of children will vary greatly. Some children will stay close to the wall and others will get farther away. This is the child's way of saying, "I want to be successful," or, "I am ready for a challenge."

Overhand Target Throw

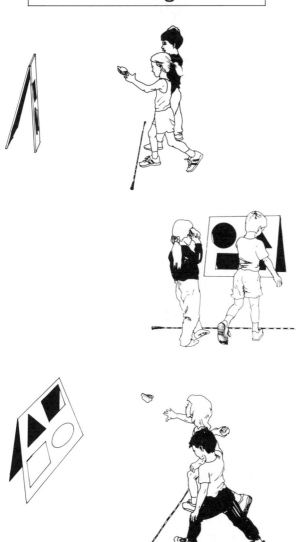

Throwing instructions for the target board throw are similar to the wall throw.

Instruction:

"Place the beanbag in your hand, hold your throwing hand and beanbag behind and to the side of your head, step forward on the opposite foot, then move the arm forward releasing the beanbag toward the target."

While all children are practicing this throw the teacher can help children having difficulty.

The use of a restraining line helps children by forcing them to stand away from the target and to throw hard to reach the target. This enables children to practice moving their throwing arm through a full range of motion. This helps develop more accurate throws. Masking tape or a jump rope placed in a straight line on the floor can be used as restraining lines. The line can be moved up or back to match a child's skill level.

Different targets can give children a focus for throwing (see Figure 10.6). A wooden stand-up target board can be used to practice both overhand and underhand throwing and can be easily moved around the classroom. It also takes little storage space.

Wooden targets can be constructed from 3/4-inch plywood. Cut a 32-inch square for the target surface, and cut different-shaped holes in the board—circle, square, triangle, rectangle. Supports are constructed so that the target leans back slightly and so that the

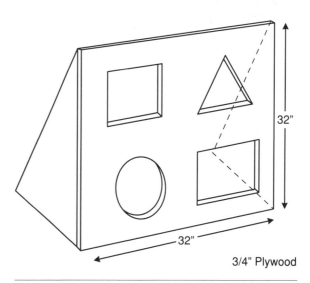

Figure 10.6 Constructing a target board.

bottom of the supports are wider than the tops. This allows the target to be used for both overhand and underhand throws. Attach supports to the target with nails and glue.

Underhand Target Throw

Throwing underhand basically requires the same stepping pattern as the overhand throw. When throwing, the child should step forward on the opposite foot. In the underhand throw, the arm and hand start at the side of the body, and as the child steps forward with the opposite foot, the throwing arm swings first back then forward, releasing the beanbag toward the target.

Across-Body Throw

The across-body throw uses a different stepping motion than the overhand and underhand throws and may confuse young children. Throwing a Frisbee is a good example of an across-the-body throwing motion: The object is thrown across the front of the body while the thrower steps with the foot on the throwing hand side. For practicing indoors, a foam disc is more appropriate. It can be cut 1 inch thick and 8 to 12 inches in diameter.

Instruction:

"Hold the disc so your thumb is on top and your fingers are on the bottom. Keep the disc lying flat like a plate. Before throwing, cross the disc in front of the body, then move your arm forward and release the disc in front of your body."

Throwing is difficult for preschool children to master. It may take months for children to learn to step with the opposite foot, so teachers should concentrate on developing that throwing pattern.

Catching

Catching is receiving and controlling an object by the body or its parts (Graham et al., 1987). As children learn to catch, they may fear the ball and pull away to protect themselves. Eventually, children will develop their catching skills and their fears will subside.

Children progress from catching a ball with their whole body, then with their arms and hands, and eventually with their hands alone.

Catching Cues
Cues for children to focus on when attempting to catch: 1. Watch the ball. 2. Get hands and arms in position to catch. 3. Reach for the ball.

Catching Activities

As I said earlier, punchball balloons are excellent for helping children develop catching skills. Because throwing and catching skills cannot always be dealt with individually, balloon catching activities were included with the balloon throwing activities at the beginning of this chapter, page 63.

Scarf Catching

Catching a scarf is a good learning device because the scarf moves slowly through the air giving children plenty of time to prepare for a catch.

Equipment:

Scarves can be purchased or can be made from a 12-inch square of lightweight material. Tissues and paper towels are good alternatives.

Instruction:

"Hold the scarf in your hand and down to your side. With an underhand throwing motion, raise your arm and release the scarf into the air. Throw hard so that the scarf goes high. Can you reach out and catch the scarf?" Children may need a teacher's help to throw the scarf.

Catching With Launch Boards

Catching Travel Map

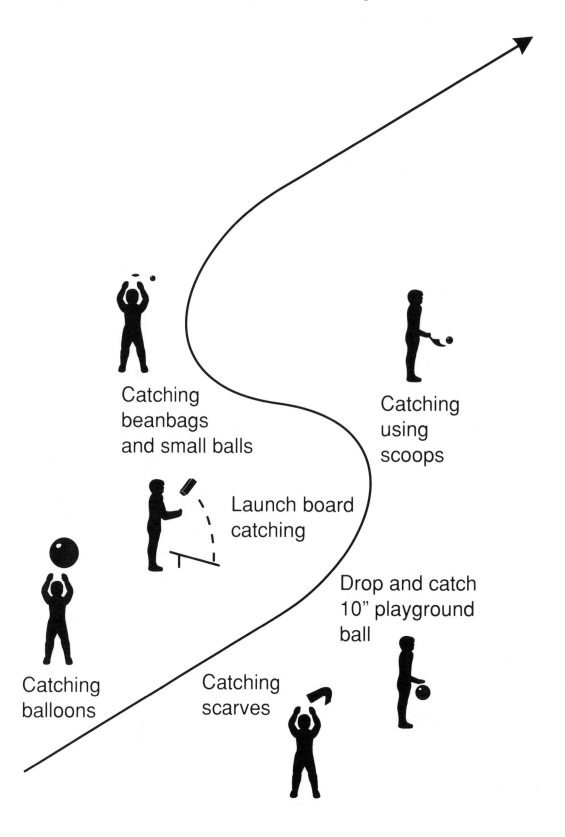

Catching
beanbags
and small balls

Catching
using
scoops

Launch board
catching

Drop and catch
10" playground
ball

Catching
balloons

Catching
scarves

Figure 10.7

The main reason it is difficult for young children to *catch* well is because they don't yet *throw* well. To catch a ball, the child must throw the ball into the air, find it in the air, track it with the eyes, and position the body and hands for a catch. Many young children just can't combine all of those skills.

A great way to help children achieve catching success is to use a launch board. When a child steps on one end of the board, a beanbag on the other end flies into the air directly in front of the child. This gives the child a good chance to catch the beanbag.

Equipment:

Launch boards are easy to make. (See Figure 10.8.) Use 1/4-inch-thick birch plywood, 30 inches long and 5 inches wide. Seven inches from one end, attach a 5-inch-long, 1-1/2-inch-diameter dowel stick with glue and screws.

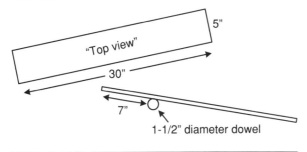

Figure 10.8   Constructing a launch board.

Place a small ball or beanbag on the launch end of the board. If using a ball, drill a 2-inch hole in the end of the board to lay the ball in. A cubed beanbag works well because it easily fits into a child's small hands.

Instruction:

"Place your beanbag on the low end of the board. Go to the other end, get your hands ready to catch by holding them out in front of you, then raise your foot and stomp on the end of the board. As the beanbag flies into the air in front of you, clap your hands around the beanbag and catch it."

Most children will have trouble coordinating the acts of picking up the foot and stomping on the board. They may stomp in the wrong place or miss completely. It helps to draw an *X* or paint a child's footprint on the board as a target.

As children get better at catching they can be challenged with more difficult tasks. "See how high you can make the beanbag go and still catch it." Or, "See how many times you can clap your hands while the beanbag is in the air and still catch it."

Catching Ghosts

A fun idea is to give children some "ghosts" to catch. Lay a beanbag on one end of the launch board with a scarf over it. As the child stomps the board, the ghost (scarf) will fly into the air. The child then tries to catch the ghost.

Instruction:

"Can you catch the ghost before it hits the ground?"

Scoop Catch

A scoop can help children who still can't quite catch with their hands. The scoop serves as an extension of the child's hand and makes it easier to catch.

Equipment:

Scoops can be purchased from physical education supply companies (Appendix A) or can be made from gallon plastic milk jugs. Cut out the bottom of the jug, hold the handle, and you have a scoop. (See Figure 10.9.)

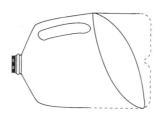

Figure 10.9   Constructing a scoop from a gallon milk jug.

Instruction:

"Hold your scoop out in front of you, stomp the beanbag into the air, and move the scoop under the beanbag to catch it. How high can you stomp the beanbag and still catch it?"

After children master catching one beanbag, they can be challenged to catch two or more beanbags in the scoop.

Instruction:

"Place the beanbags long ways on the end of the board, stomp the board, and while the beanbags are in the air move your scoop in position to catch the beanbags." Because the beanbags were laid long ways on the board they will rise to different heights. This means that children will be catching the beanbags one at a time.

What Can I Catch Now?

Do not limit your students to catching beanbags. After some skills have been developed using beanbags, propel other catchable objects (small stuffed animals or Ethafoam bowling pins) into the air.

Two-Beanbag Catch

Catching Ethafoam Pins

Equipment:

Ethafoam bowling pins can be purchased through physical education supply companies (Appendix A). The pins are lightweight, safe, and easy to catch. One-liter plastic bottles are good replacements for Ethafoam pins. Using the foam pins with the launch boards lets children imagine that they are shooting rockets to the Moon.

Instruction:

"Place your rocket on the rocket launcher and start your countdown, '3, 2, 1, blast off.' As the rocket flies into the air get your hands and body ready to catch it when it returns to Earth."

Additional challenges include laying the rocket on its side on the board and stomping it into the air to catch, or rolling the pin from the top of the board and, when it reaches the bottom of the board, stomping it into the air and catching it.

Catching skills are difficult for young children to master. Practice using scarves, balloons, and launch boards to give children a good base from which to develop skills. For instance, we want children to progress such that they can catch balls thrown to them. But that is difficult to do in preschool because most children are not ready to throw and catch with a partner.

To the Teacher's Credit

Pat yourself on the back if at the end of the school year the children you teach

- step on the opposite foot when throwing;
- get their hands and bodies ready when attempting to catch a ball;
- keep their eyes on the ball when attempting to catch; and
- are having fun and participating.

High Skilled Catching

Skilled children should be challenged to catch with both hands.

Instruction:

"Place two beanbags side by side on the board. Hold your hands in front of you with palms facing up and forward so that you can grab the beanbags out of the air. Then stomp on the board sending the beanbags into the air and catch one beanbag in each hand."

Chapter 11

Striking With Body Parts (Volleying and Dribbling)

Striking skills are part of many games. Striking can mean striking with body parts or striking with implements. Striking with body parts can be divided into volleying, dribbling, punting, and kicking. This chapter concentrates on volleying and dribbling. The action in all these forms of striking is the same: to propel an object away from the body with a hit, punch, or tap (Graham et al., 1987).

Volleying is striking an object with a body part—hands, head, elbows, or knees. Dribbling is volleying that involves striking downward, usually with the hands.

Volleying and Dribbling Cues

Focusing on the ball will help children succeed in both volleying and dribbling. An additional cue when presenting volleying is to have children strike the ball or balloon with a flat body surface. If, for example, the child's hand is angled and not flat when striking, the ball will fly off at an angle and not go straight up. A ball hit straight is easier to hit a second time.

In dribbling, the focus is on striking the ball down with the tips of the fingers ("finger pads"). Children who dribble with the palms of their hands have trouble keeping the ball in front of them and under control. Children should not dribble the ball above the knees; a ball dribbled

(Cont.)

higher is harder to control. Without this focus, children may spend more time chasing balls than developing dribbling skills.

Striking Activities

Large punchball balloons—which move slowly and give children time to track them and prepare the body to strike (Figure 11.1)—are excellent for helping young children develop striking skills. Frequent practice helps children achieve the hand-eye coordination used in games involving striking.

Figure 11.1 Use large punchball balloons to teach children striking skills.

Volleying and Dribbling Travel Map

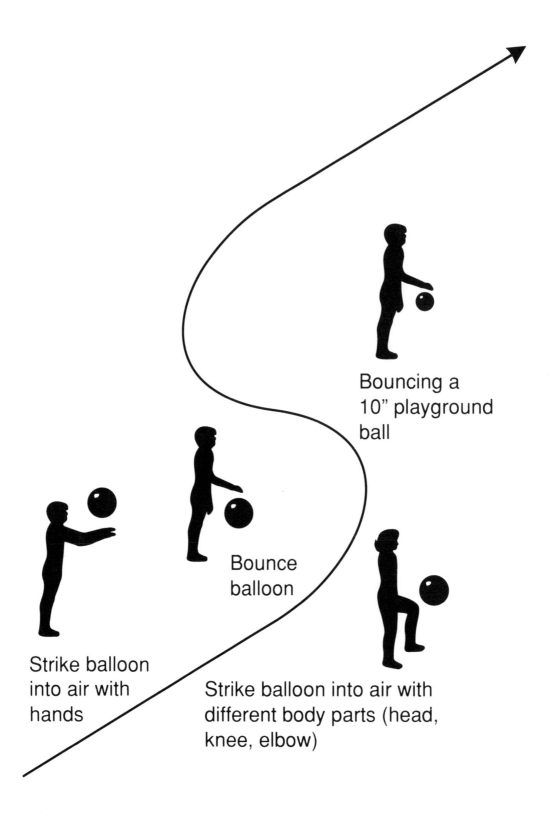

Bouncing a
10" playground
ball

Bounce
balloon

Strike balloon
into air with
hands

Strike balloon into air with
different body parts (head,
knee, elbow)

Figure 11.2

These balloons can be purchased at most local toy stores for less than $1. Smaller balloons (not as thick and durable) are not recommended. Blow the balloon up to a 16-inch diameter. After filling the balloon with air, tightly roll the end of the balloon and then poke the rolled end into the balloon. This allows you to blow the balloon up again if air comes out. Tying a knot in the end of the balloon lessens your ability to add air later.

Striking Balloons

The first step in striking the balloon is to throw it into the air. Children can consistently throw the balloon straight up into the air if they follow this instruction.

Instruction:

"Hold the balloon in both hands and lower the balloon so that it almost touches your knees. Raise both hands into the air and let go of the balloon as it passes your nose."

Next, ask children to "look up so you can see the balloon." They can't succeed at striking the balloon without visually tracking it. "When the balloon comes down, hit it back into the air with your hands."

Children should practice striking with one hand and then with two. In the beginning, just making contact with the balloon will be an accomplishment worthy of the teacher's praise. Remember that striking a balloon with the hands may be difficult for a young child.

Striking With One Hand

Children need to learn two striking patterns: underhand and overhand. The underhand motion begins by placing arms and hands in front of the body with palms up. To strike, children raise arms and contact the balloon with hands and fingers. It is easier in the beginning to strike with one hand. Many children cannot coordinate striking with two.

Striking With Two Hands

The overhand pattern is like a player striking a volleyball above the head. Begin with arms and hands above the head with palms up and elbows bent. When the balloon comes down raise both arms and contact the balloon with both hands. Jumping when the balloon is struck propels the balloon higher into the air.

Striking With the Head

Teach children to use more than their hands while they develop striking skills. Children respond well to the challenge of striking with other body parts, especially with the head. This skill requires children to track the balloon, to position their bodies under the balloon, and to jump at the appropriate time.

Instruction:

"Can you throw the balloon into the air, jump, and strike the balloon with your head? Make sure you look up and keep your eyes on the balloon [cue]."

Using Different Body Parts

Children also should be taught to strike with their elbows, shoulders, and knees. Children may also have their own ideas.

Instruction:

"Which body parts can you think of to use to strike the balloon?" Remember to emphasize striking with a flat body surface.

High Skilled Striking

After children develop basic skills, ask them to see how many times they can strike the balloon without missing.

Instruction:

"Can you strike the balloon into the air five times without letting it touch the floor? Ten times? Twenty times?" By age 5 most children can strike a balloon into the air from 5 to 50 straight times.

"Can you keep the balloon in the air by striking it each time with a different body part?" You may need to be more specific. "Can you strike the balloon into the air first with your hand, then with your head, then with your elbow, then with your knee, and finally with your hand again? Can you keep this pattern going?"

Dribbling

Children love to bounce a ball, and lightweight balloons are excellent for introducing that skill. Rubber playground balls or regulation basketballs, which are too heavy for young children to dribble successfully, can frustrate children and defeat the desire to practice the skill. Remind your students to dribble the balloon by touching it only with their fingertips and not other parts of their hands.

Instruction:

Ask children to "hold the balloon in front of your body, drop the balloon, and when the balloon bounces up use your fingertips to gently strike the balloon back down to the floor. Keep striking the balloon down softly and see how many times you can bounce the balloon without stopping."

Children who succeed in bouncing a balloon are ready to bounce a ball. Teachers must judge when students are ready for more difficult activities. Use an instruction much like your instruction for bouncing the balloon. "Drop the ball, and when it bounces up strike down gently with your finger pads. You will have to strike down harder than you did with the balloons." Children should experiment with both soft and hard dribbles, but will delight in seeing how hard and how high they can bounce the ball. If children have trouble bouncing balls, go back to balloons and review the motions.

When children can dribble standing still, challenge them to dribble while walking.

Chapter 12

Kicking and Punting

Many games include kicking and punting. Kicking requires that children contact a ball with their foot while maintaining the balance necessary to propel the ball as straight and as far as they desire.

Punting is a form of kicking, but is harder to master. It requires dropping the ball, raising the kicking leg, and striking the ball with the foot before the ball can fall to the ground.

Kicking Cues

Stress these cues when children are learning to kick.
1. Look at the ball when kicking.
2. Place nonkicking foot next to ball.
3. Contact the ball with the inside middle part of the foot.

Pick one, and only one, cue for the children to work on at a time. After children learn to look at the ball when kicking, they can concentrate on another cue. Asking children to concentrate on too many cues at one time is confusing.

Kicking and Punting Activities

Punchball balloons are excellent for children to use when developing beginning kicking and punting skills. In the beginning, emphasize simply making contact with the balloon—not where the balloon travels.

Kick the Balloon

First, have children kick a stationary punchball balloon.

Instruction:

"Lay your balloon on the floor in front of you, place your nonkicking foot beside the balloon, and kick it as hard as you can. Now take a couple of steps away from the balloon and then walk up and kick the balloon. Let's concentrate on kicking the balloon with the inside part of your foot. Walk forward and kick the balloon as hard as you can."

Teacher's Note:

Ask children to kick the balloon hard so they practice moving their kicking leg fully from back to front.

Kicking and Punting Travel Map

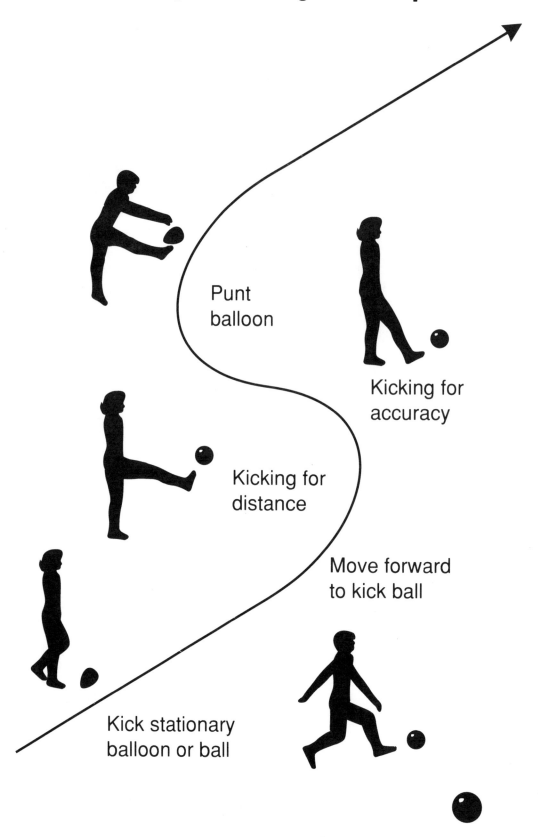

Punt balloon

Kicking for accuracy

Kicking for distance

Move forward to kick ball

Kick stationary balloon or ball

Figure 12.1

Kick the Ball

Ten-inch-diameter rubber playground balls and foam soccer balls are both appropriate for young children when they advance from kicking the balloon. It is best to practice kicking these heavier balls outdoors in an area large enough so children do not accidentally kick a ball into another child.

Children should first kick a stationary ball without a step, then they should take a couple of steps before kicking. Emphasize stepping with the opposite foot and kicking with the inside of the foot.

Distance Kick

Place traffic cones 10 to 15 yards away from the children as a kicking target. Stress kicking for distance before kicking for accuracy.

Instruction:

Ask each child to place a ball on the ground and step back about "three big steps." Then say, "Show me how far you can kick the ball."

Accuracy Kick

Set two traffic cones about 6 feet apart, and ask the children to stay behind a line 5 to 8 feet from the cones. As accuracy improves, move the cones closer together and move the line farther from the targets.

Instruction:

"Can you kick the ball between the two cones?"

Punting Cues
Stress these cues as children learn to punt:
1. Look at the ball at all times.
2. Step forward on the nonkicking foot.
3. Contact the ball with the top of the foot (on your shoestrings).

Punt the Balloon

As a rule, preschool children are not successful punting a football or playground ball because the balls are too heavy. Preschool children should practice punting the balloons until teachers determine they can punt a heavier ball. This usually happens in elementary school.

Instruction:

"Hold the balloon in both hands with your arms straight out in front of your body. Release the balloon so that it drops down and a little forward. Raise your kicking foot and kick the balloon before it touches the ground. Make sure you kick the balloon with the top of your foot; kick it with your shoestrings [cue]."

Chapter 13

Striking With Paddles

Striking with a paddle calls on children to coordinate several familiar skills into one smooth motion. Children must toss or drop a ball, visually track it, and contact the ball at the right moment. The child also must adjust to the weight and length of the paddle.

Cues for Striking With Paddles
Use these cues to help children strike with a paddle: 1. Look at the ball when striking and watch the ball as it moves toward the paddle. 2. Make contact with the ball with the middle of the paddle. 3. Keep your feet stationary when swinging the paddle.

Suggested Equipment

You'll need an Ethafoam paddle, a balloon, a small plastic ball, and an 18-inch-high traffic cone (chapter 3).

Striking Activities

Children should practice striking a stationary ball before trying to hit a moving ball. Because striking with an implement is complex, children should first be able to strike with body parts, especially with their hands.

Smack the Balloon

Instruction:

"Place your balloon on the floor in front of you. Hold your paddle in one hand at your side. Swing your arm forward and smack the balloon as hard as you can. Let's see how far we can make the balloon travel."

Toss and Strike

Ask children to hold their balloons out in front of their bodies, supporting the balloons

Striking With Paddles Travel Map

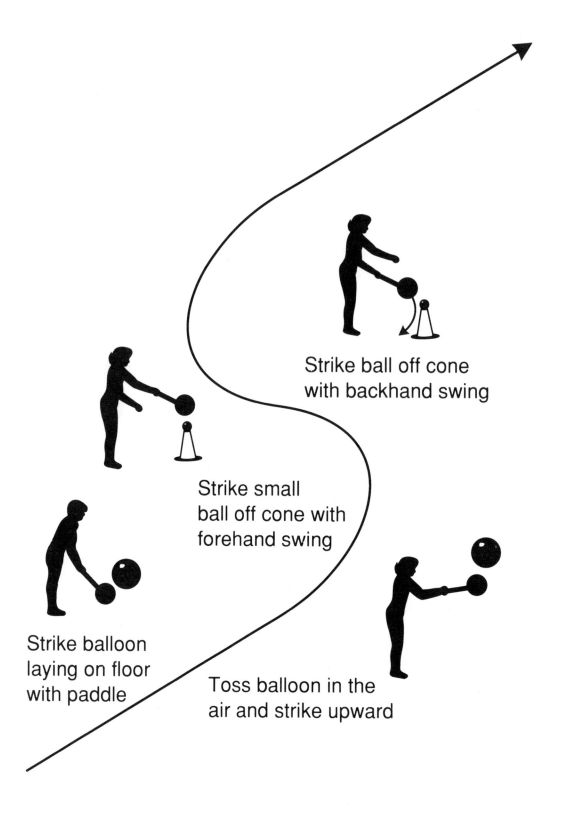

Strike ball off cone
with backhand swing

Strike small
ball off cone with
forehand swing

Strike balloon
laying on floor
with paddle

Toss balloon in the
air and strike upward

Figure 13.1

on one side with their hands and on the other side with the paddles they are holding.

Instruction:

"Can you throw the balloon high into the air and when it comes down strike it with the paddle?"

Note:

The upward swinging motion used in striking with the hands should be used when striking with the paddle. The same cue also should be used: Keep a flat striking surface, in this case a flat paddle.

The first thing we want to teach about striking with a paddle is to make contact with a stationary ball. An easy way to help young children develop their forehand and backhand striking skills (skills used in tennis or racquetball) is to use an 18-inch-high traffic cone, a paddle, and a plastic ball. This is the same principle as using a batting tee to teach a child to hit a baseball.

If indoors, make sure children can swing the paddles without hitting others. A foam tennis ball may be better to use indoors than a plastic ball.

Children who can't easily strike a tossed ball can let the balloon bounce on the floor before they strike it. Challenge children with experience to strike the balloon with more force and in different directions. Children can strike a balloon into the air with the paddle from 5 to 50 times without stopping.

Instruction:

"Place your ball on the cone. Hold your paddle to the side of your body and strike the ball as hard as you can." Ask children to focus on the ball and to stand still when swinging the paddle.

For the backhand, the child stands on the opposite side of the cone, holding the paddle as in the forehand. "Cross the paddle in front of your body and swing your arm forward, making contact with the ball. The swinging motion is similar to the arm action when throwing a disc."

Chapter 14

Striking With Long-Handled Implements

Adults strike with long-handled implements in many common games—baseball, hockey, and golf for instance. Because they are difficult, these usually are the last skills children develop. The length of the striking implement and the complex eye-hand coordination involved in making contact with the ball is hard for most children to master. Activities in this chapter may or may not be appropriate to the skill levels of the children you teach. To be sure, children who have not gained skill in striking with body parts and striking with paddles are not ready to strike with long-handled implements.

Striking Activities

Because golf is one of the most popular recreational sports for adults, many children will grow up to play that game. But few preschool children have the coordination to strike a small golf ball with a long golf club. Introducing some lead-up activities at an early age helps children develop the swinging pattern from which they can refine their skills later in life.

Striking Cues
These cues can help children:
1. Look at the ball before swinging.
(Cont.)

2. Face the ball with the front of your body.
3. Keep your feet shoulder width apart.
4. Don't move your feet when swinging.
5. Swing as hard as you can.

Striking With a Hockey Stick

Striking with a hockey stick is an underhand striking pattern. The main idea in hockey is to keep control, not to see how far or how hard one can hit the ball. With this in mind,

Striking With Long-Handled Implements Travel Map

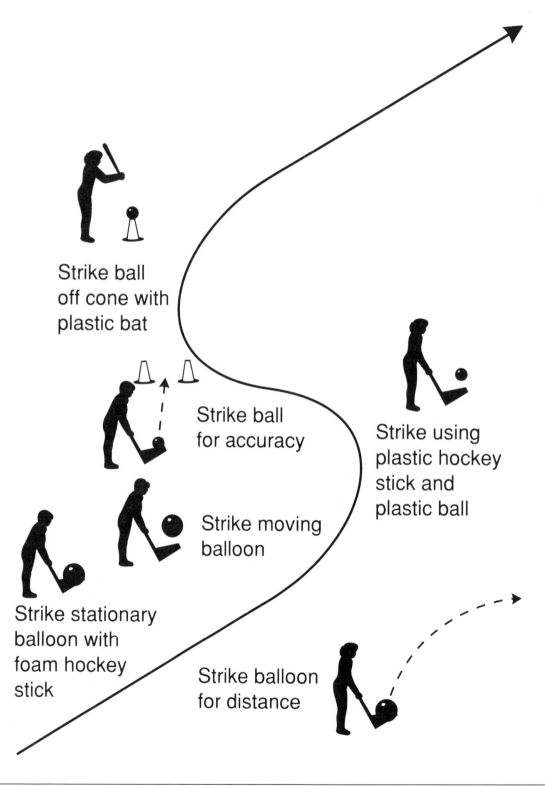

Strike ball off cone with plastic bat

Strike ball for accuracy

Strike moving balloon

Strike using plastic hockey stick and plastic ball

Strike stationary balloon with foam hockey stick

Strike balloon for distance

Figure 14.1

children should tap the ball softly and keep it close, not hit it far away. Have the children begin this exercise by striking a stationary ball, then progress to a moving ball.

Equipment:

The most appropriate equipment is a plastic hockey stick with a plastic ball, or a foam hockey stick with a punchball.

Technique:

Right-handed children hold their left hands around the tops of the sticks as if to shake hands. The right hands go just under the left. The hand placement is reversed for left-handers. Thumbs point down. (They should not hold the stick like a broom with thumbs up.) A good cue is to ask children to grip the sticks "with the hands apart." (See Figure 14.2.)

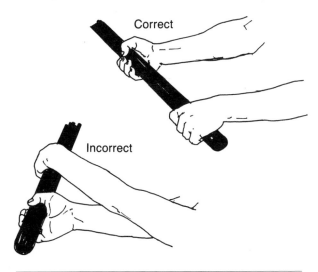

Correct

Incorrect

Figure 14.2   Correct way to hold the hockey stick. Incorrect way to hold the hockey stick.

Instruction:

"Hold the stick so that the blade is on the floor. Bring the stick back and then swing forward to strike the ball." Encourage the child to keep the blade of the stick below the waist.

Safety Note:

Children need to be careful when they swing not to strike their friends with the stick.

The Golf Swing

This outdoor activity requires a lot of space so children won't strike a classmate accidentally. This activity is safer if you use balloons and foam hockey sticks, but the golf swing can be practiced using the plastic hockey stick and ball.

Instruction:

Ask children to take a full swing with the stick and to strike the ball as hard as possible. "Plant your feet so they do not move while you swing. Bring the stick back and look down at the ball, then swing as hard as you can. Make sure to hold on to the stick so it doesn't slip from your hand."

Striking With a Bat

A horizontal swing is used when striking a ball with a bat. Preschool children should start by striking a plastic ball off a tee using a plastic bat. It helps to have children stand on a carpet square about one foot from the cone as they swing the bat. The feet should be about one foot apart with the toes pointing toward the ball and about two feet away from the ball. Improper foot position places children too close, too far away, too far in front, or too far behind the ball, and lessens their ability to hit. Placing the feet about one foot apart and keeping them "glued" to the floor balances the children and helps to keep them from falling down when they swing the bat. Remember, stress only one cue at a time.

Equipment:

Place a 3-foot-high cone or batting tee in an open area where there is no danger of children being hit accidentally with the bat. (Cones and tees can be purchased at toy or sporting goods stores. Cones are more stable and durable than tees.)

Technique:

A right-handed child places the left hand on the lowest part of the bat handle and grasps the bat with the right hand directly above the left. Hand placement is reversed for left-handers. Figure 14.3 illustrates correct and incorrect hand placement.

Instruction:

"Hold the bat back and swing as hard as you can. Make sure you look at the ball when you're swinging the bat [cue]."

Note:

Teachers can feel some accomplishment if preschool children can strike the ball off the cone (tee) in the desired direction three out of five times. Some children may be ready to have a ball thrown to them, but for most, striking the ball off a cone is itself quite an accomplishment.

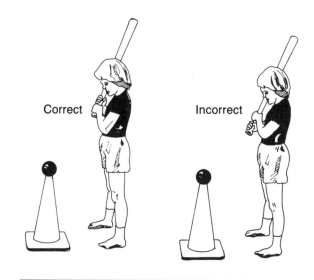

Figure 14.3 Correct and incorrect ways to hold a bat.

Chapter 15

Rhythms

Young children naturally love music. You can capitalize on that affinity by using music to explore structured rhythmic movement and to help children listen better and follow visual cues. Moving to music also helps children understand the space awareness, effort, and relationship concepts (chapter 2).

The term *rhythms* means different things to different people, traditional and cultural dance to some, creative and modern dance to others. In this curriculum, rhythmic activities deal mostly with movement of body parts either alone or with items such as rhythm sticks, ribbons, and scarves. These activities are predesigned sequences involving regular recurrence of particular movements. This activity encourages children to listen for a repeated musical pattern or beat and then to move to it.

Structured rhythmic activities using apparatus are easier to present than creative movement activities and thus make a good starting place for teachers. Teachers should be encouraged to present both this chapter's activities and creative movement activities. Some children may resist creative dance, but relish rhythmic activities where they can use rhythm sticks, scarves, or ribbon sticks. Shy or self-conscious children like using apparatus because they offer focal points on which to concentrate their movements.

Rhythmic Activities

Here are some activities to help get you started. Movements using rhythm sticks (or lum-mi sticks as they are sometimes called), ribbon sticks, scarves, and gloves are demonstrated. Select your own music or pick additional rhythmic activity music from a list in Appendix A. Two songs in chapter 5, "Tony Chestnut" and "My Head, My Shoulders, My Knees, My Toes," can be used as rhythmic activities without apparatus.

Choose music with a constant, repetitive beat slow enough for young children to follow. Teachers need to decide if movements are too difficult for their children and if the chosen music is the right tempo. Children may be unable to keep up with the music at first, but the more they perform the songs, the better their movement will become.

Rhythm Sticks

Rhythm sticks are 5/8-inch-diameter, foot-long wooden or plastic sticks that children strike together with the beat of the music.

Rhythms Travel Map

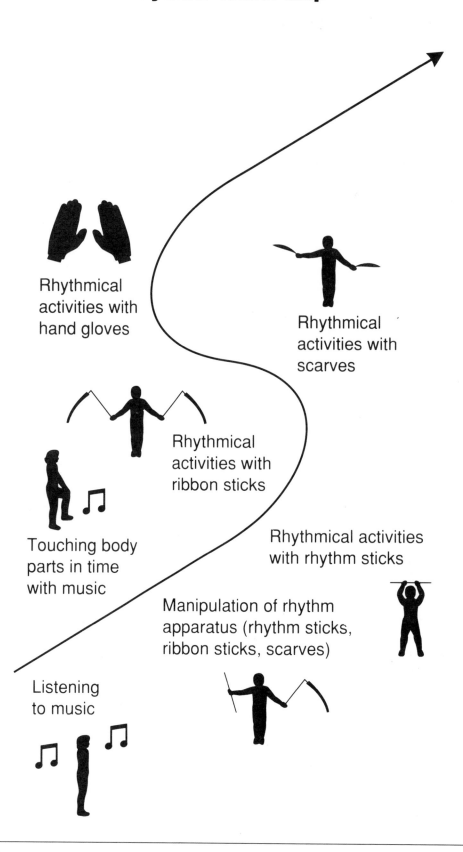

Rhythmical activities with hand gloves

Rhythmical activities with scarves

Rhythmical activities with ribbon sticks

Touching body parts in time with music

Rhythmical activities with rhythm sticks

Manipulation of rhythm apparatus (rhythm sticks, ribbon sticks, scarves)

Listening to music

Figure 15.1

Sticks can be purchased (Appendix A) or made (Figure 15.2) from wooden dowel sticks. If you make sticks, be sure they are sanded so children do not get splinters in their hands. Sticks can be painted to help children identify colors.

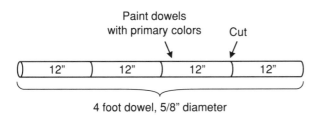

Figure 15.2   Making rhythm sticks.

Give your children plenty of space so they don't accidentally hit another child with a stick. Ask children to get two sticks and to sit on their carpet squares in a large circle.

Several activities can be practiced without music and teach children to move with the rhythm sticks.

Drums

Instruction:

"Can you use your sticks like drum sticks and play the drum?" (Children strike the sticks on the floor as if playing a drum.) "Can you play the drum softly?" "Can you play the drum hard?" Ask children to first play hard then soft so they can begin to understand the difference. Children learn this concept quickly (see chapter 2).

Down and Together

Instruction:

"Let's put the drum beat and striking sticks together in a pattern. Can you strike the sticks down and then together, down—together—down—together? Strike the sticks first down on the floor to your side then together in front of you."

Hammer

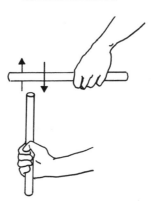

Instruction:

"Let's build a house using one stick for the 'nail' and the other stick for the 'hammer'. Hold the nail straight up with one end on the floor and strike the other end with your hammer. Be careful not to hit your hand with the hammer."

Peel the Carrot

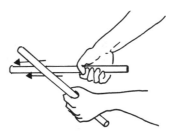

Instruction:

"We have been working so hard that I am getting hungry. Let's peel a carrot for lunch.'' (While holding the sticks, one in each hand, scrape the sticks together as if peeling a carrot.)

Tower

Instruction:

"Now we are going to build a tower. Hold one stick upright with one end on the floor. Place the other stick upright with one end on top of the first stick. Can you blow your tower down?''

Letters

Instruction:

"Let's use our sticks to make letters. Can you make a *T* with your sticks? Can you make an *X* or a *V*?''

Rhythm Roundup

Here are two songs as examples of dozens of possibilities. Teachers may want to use the class's favorite song with rhythmic sticks.

"Michael Finnegan"

"Michael Finnegan" starts with children sitting in a circle on carpet squares. First, they hammer, then strike the sticks four times (beginning in front of the child and then above the child's head). Finally, the child strikes the stick down on the floor and then together in front of the body. The song and accompanying movements are repeated three times. Here are the words to the song and the pattern in which children should strike their rhythm sticks:

Lyrics

There was an old man named Michael Finnegan,
(*Hammer,   2,   3,   4*)
He grew whiskers on his chinnegan,
(*5,   6,   7,   8*)
Shaved them off but they grew in again,
(*Up,   2,   3,   4*)
Poor old Michael Finnegan. Begin again.
(*Down,   cross,   down,   cross*)
(*Repeat*)

"When the Saints Go Marching In"

In this favorite, children march as they strike sticks together to the beat of the music. The progression includes striking the sticks in front of the body while marching in place, in back of the body, above the head, to the side, below the waist, and then to the other side. Finish by marching in place and striking sticks to the beat. New movements can be made up for other verses. Here are the words and (in parentheses) rhythmic directions:

Lyrics

Oh, when the saints go marching in,
(*March, 2, 3, 4, 5, 6, 7, 8*)
Oh, when the saints go marching in,
(*Back, 2, 3, 4, 5, 6, 7, 8*)
Oh, Lord, I want to be in that number,
(*Tap up,   side,   down,   side*)
When the saints go marching in.
(*In place, 3, 4, 5, 6, 7, 8*)

Oh, when the stars refuse to shine,
(*Tap across,   2,   3,   4*)
Oh, when the stars refuse to shine,
(*Again,   2,   3,   4*)

Oh, Lord, I want to be in that number,
(*Tap up,   side,   down,   side*)
When the stars refuse to shine.
(*In place, 3, 4, 5, 6, 7, 8*)

Oh, when I hear that trumpet sound,
(*Circle right, 3, 4, 5, 6, 7, 8*)

Oh, when I hear that trumpet sound,
(*Circle left, 3, 4, 5, 6, 7, 8*)

Oh, Lord, I want to be in that number,
(*Tap up,   side,   down,   side*)
When I hear that trumpet sound.
(*In place, 3, 4, 5, 6, 7, 8*)

Ribbon Stick Activities

Ribbon stick activities are used to emphasize the different pathways (curved, circu-
lar, straight, or zigzag) around the body.

To make ribbon sticks (Figure 15.3) you
will need 18-inch-long, 1/4-inch-diameter
wooden dowel sticks, a double-sided fish
swivel, some fishing line, and 9 feet of cloth
ribbon 1-1/2 inches wide. Drill a small hole
in one end of the stick and attach the fish
swivel to the stick using approximately 4
inches of fishing line. Fold over one end of
the ribbon about 1/4-inch and sew it to keep
it from unraveling. Fold over the other end
of the ribbon and sew onto it a 1-inch square
of cardboard, similar to a note pad backing.
This keeps the ribbon from tangling. When
you sew the cardboard onto the ribbon, include a piece of fishing line, which you attach to the swivel. The ribbon stick is now
completed.

Make sure children understand they need
to avoid hitting others with the ribbons.
(Move the children's carpet squares farther
apart.)

Before moving the ribbons to music, practice these movements without music.

| **Wipers** |

In this movement, patterned after the motion of windshield wipers, children move
their hands and arms from right to left as
the ribbon flows back and forth high in the
air.

| **Circles** |

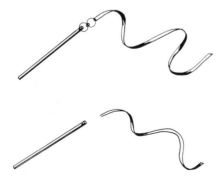

Figure 15.3 Constructing a ribbon stick.

Instruction:

"Hold the end of the stick and move your hand and arm in a large circle in front of your body. Can you make circles at your side? Can you make a circle over your head?"

Children use the ribbon stick as a fishing pole. They move the stick into the air and slightly behind the head, then bring the hand and arm forward as if throwing a fishing line into the lake. Next they bring the line back over their heads and begin again. They should practice this movement several times.

Floor Sweeps

Squiggle Down

Instruction:

"Move your ribbon from side to side on the floor in front of you. Can you pretend that you are sweeping the floor?"

This movement is similar to fishing except when children bring the ribbon forward they should shake it in a zigzag path from above their heads down to the floor.

Fishing

Snakes

This movement is seldom used with a song, but children do love to watch the ribbon move like a snake on the floor.

Instruction:

"Can you move the ribbon back and forth on the floor like a snake?"

Flags

Use music as an accompaniment as children march throughout the room while waving ribbons like flags from side to side above their heads.

Ribbon Roundup

"Michael Row the Boat" and "Kookaburra" are two of many songs you can use to accompany children's ribbon movements. You might want to choose one of the group's favorite songs.

"Michael Row the Boat"

Michael row the boat ashore, Hallelujah
(*Wipers, 2, 3, 4, up, down, up, down*)

Michael row the boat ashore, Hallelujah
(*Wipers, 2, 3, 4, up, down, up, down*)

Gabriel, blow the trumpet horn, Hallelujah
(*Sweeps, 2, 3, 4, up, down, up, down*)

Gabriel, blow the trumpet horn, Hallelujah
(*Sweeps, 2, 3, 4, up, down, up, down*)

Michael got a music boat, Hallelujah
(*Circle, 2, 3, 4, up, down, up, down*)

Michael got a music boat, Hallelujah
(*Circle, 2, 3, 4, up, down, up, down*)

Brother, lend a helping hand, Hallelujah
(*Wipers, 2, 3, 4, up, down, up, down*)

Brother, lend a helping hand, Hallelujah
(*Wipers, 2, 3, 4, up, down, up, down*)

Jordan stream is deep and wide, Hallelujah
(*Sweeps, 2, 3, 4, up, down, up, down*)

Jordan stream is deep and wide, Hallelujah
(*Sweeps, 2, 3, 4, up, down, up, down*)

Michael row the boat ashore, Hallelujah
(*Circle, 2, 3, 4, up, down, up, down*)

Michael row the boat ashore, Hallelujah
(*Circle, 2, 3, 4, up, down, up, down*)

"Kookaburra"

Kookaburra sits in an old gum tree
(*Circle, 2, 3, 4, 5, 6, 7, 8*)

Merry merry king of the bush is he
(*Circle, 2, 3, 4, 5, 6, 7, 8*)

Laugh Kookaburra, Laugh Kookaburra
(*Up, squiggle, up, squiggle*)

Gay your life must be.
(*Circle, 2, 3, 4*)

Repeat song using wipers and sweeps, and finish with circles.

Scarves

Scarves are used as props much as are ribbon sticks: to help children learn about the pathways surrounding their bodies. You can buy scarves or make them by cutting lightweight material into 16-inch squares. Lightweight material will float gently through the air. A paper towel is an inexpensive alternative. Hold the scarf by a corner when moving it through the air.

Wipers

Move a scarf in front of the body in a pattern similar to windshield wipers.

Floor Sweeps

Move a scarf back and forth as if sweeping the floor.

Circles

Move a scarf in large circles in front, to the side, and overhead.

Fishing

Move a scarf in front of the body as if throwing a fishing line into a lake and then pulling it back.

Flags

Gallop around the room while waving a scarf in the air like a flag.

Scarf Roundup

"Yankee Doodle" and "Shoo Fly" are among the songs you can use for activities with scarves.

"Yankee Doodle"

Yankee Doodle went to town a riding on a pony
(*Wipers, 2, 3, 4, 5, 6, 7, 8*)

He stuck a feather in his hat and called it macaroni
(*Up, down, 2, 3, 4, 5, 6, 7, 8*)

Yankee Doodle keep it up, Yankee Doodle dandy
(*Gallop, 2, 3, 4, 5, 6, 7, 8*)

Mind the music and the step and with the girls be handy.
(*Reverse, 2, 3, 4, 5, 6, 7, 8*)

Repeat twice, using sweeps, then circles in place of wipers.

"Shoo Fly"

Shoo fly, don't bother me
(*Wave, wave, wiper, wiper*)

Shoo fly, don't bother me
(*Wave, wave, wiper, wiper*)

Shoo fly, don't bother me
(*Wave, wave, wiper, wiper*)

For I belong to somebody
(*Circle, 2, 3, 4*)

I feel, I feel, I feel,
(*Up, 2, 3, 4*)

I feel like a morning star
(*Circle, 2, 3, 4*)

I feel, I feel, I feel,
(*Down, 2, 3, 4*)

I feel like a morning star.
(*Circle, 2, 3, 4*)

Repeat twice.

Hand Dancing

Children have moved their hands to a musical beat for generations. In the '70s, the movie "Grease" inspired thousands of young people, from elementary school through high school, to do the "hand jive."

Hand dancing is especially popular with elementary school children because they and a partner can create their own sequences of hand movements. Hand dancing while wearing gloves is more fun for children and helps the children focus on the hands. Gloves should fit the child's hands but not fit so tight they restrict movement.

Keep the movements within preschoolers' abilities and remember that the music should be slow enough that children can easily move to the beat.

Here are some hand-dancing skills you can introduce to children:

1. One hand up
2. Both hands up
3. One hand waves
4. Both hands wave
5. One hand points
6. Both hands point
7. Index finger up and down

It will help children to rehearse hand-dancing skills (especially movements to a particular song) before attempting a song. "This Old Man" and "Bingo" are among the many good songs for hand dancing.

"This Old Man"

This old man, he played one
(*Hold up one finger and wave back and forth*)

He played nick nack on my drum
(*Point up, up, down, down*)

Nick nack paddy whack
(*Clap, clap*)

Give a dog a bone
(*Wave, wave*)

This old man came rolling home
(*Roll hands*)

(*Note: Repeat this verse 9 times, changing the numbers in each verse.*)

"Bingo"

There was a farmer had a dog
(*Right hand up, left hand up*)

And Bingo was his name-o
(*Right hand wave, left hand wave*)

B - I - N - G - O
(*Slap, clap, together, together*)

B - I - N - G - O
(*Slap, clap, together, together*)

B - I - N - G - O
(*Slap, clap, together, together*)

And Bingo was his name-o
(*Right hand point up, left hand point up*)

(*Note: Perform the same verse five times.*)

Part III

Organizing Movement Activities Into a Curriculum

Chapter 16

Lesson Planning

Planning—the most essential part of designing a movement curriculum—enables teachers to logically present a curriculum appropriate to developing basic skills in young children.

This chapter provides a blueprint, a lesson plan (Appendix C) that guides you through movement activities in earlier chapters. Lesson plans consist of travel map activities; skill themes and concepts to be stressed; a suggested time limit for each activity; suggested equipment for each activity; and a suggested order in which to present activities. Each lesson plan also states the children's learning target for the class—both review of skills previously introduced and new skills. A final section of the form focuses on what the teacher should watch for.

Eight 30-minute lesson plans are included, a number based on classes meeting once a week for 30 minutes. At the end of the eight-week period, start over with Lesson 1. Although skill themes may be revisited every 8 weeks, you need not present the same activities. Instead, move forward or backward on the travel maps and present different activities. For example, chapter 10 suggests a progression of throwing and catching activities based on children's achievement levels. Lesson plans in this chapter are arranged to match those levels. During the first 8 weeks, teachers begin at the bottom of the travel maps. But teachers will start the next 8-week set of plans one skill level higher up the travel map. Teachers may want to move up and down the travel maps to add new activities and revisit old ones. They may be ready to create their own plans after going through eight lessons.

Each weekly plan divides skill themes into locomotor, nonmanipulative, and manipulative skills. The idea is to present activities from each area during every class. The more the activities are presented, the better the chance children will develop the skills you desire.

The plan also tells you how long you can spend on each activity within a 30-minute period. Teachers with shorter or longer classes can make appropriate adjustments. Teachers also may want to adjust the number of activities during each class to meet their own teaching pace. These lesson plans are examples only. Only you can judge what is appropriate to your setting. Do not be too concerned, for instance, if you do not get through every activity in each lesson. If children like jumping rope, let them practice as long as they show interest. If you miss an activity one week, add it to the next.

Basic movement skills do not develop in children by accident. A plan that gives order to skill themes and movement concepts, especially fun activities, motivates children to develop basic skills. Teachers may want to review the example of Mrs. Phillips' first movement class (chapter 2) if they have questions about presenting activities.

Determining How Much Time to Spend on Skill Themes

To help teachers create their own lesson plans, here are suggested percentages of time to spend on each skill theme during the school year. These guidelines, designed to give teachers a starting place, reflect years of experience working with children. These percentages can help you determine which skill themes young children should work on most and in what order to help them develop physical skills. Teachers can apply the percentages to chapter activities and travel maps.

Locomotor skills and establishing the environment	17%
Body part identification	3%
Jumping and landing	12%
Rolling	8%
Balance	15%
Throwing and catching	12%
Striking with body parts	8%
Kicking and punting	6%
Striking with paddles	6%
Striking with long-handled implements	3%
Rhythms	10%

Lesson 1

Time: 30 minutes

Equipment: Stop and go signals (drum, sticks), beanbags, jump boxes, punchball balloons, hoops, and music ("My Head, My Shoulders, My Knees, My Toes")

In this lesson children learn space awareness concepts of general and self-space; locomotor skills of walking, marching, galloping, and hopping; jumping with two-foot takeoffs and two-foot landings, emphasizing swinging the arms; different body parts; how to throw a punchball balloon straight into the air; where to place arms to best catch the balloon; and striking with a flat body part.

Travel Maps: Locomotor skills, jumping, body awareness, throwing, catching, striking with body parts

Note: Rhythm activities are not suggested at the beginning of the first two classes. These are new experiences for children, and initial classes should emphasize developing the movement environment.

Locomotor Activities (10 minutes)

1. Introduce concepts of general and self-space and establish the movement environment (chapter 4).
Q. Does everyone understand where the boundaries are and what self-space and general space mean? Are children moving through the environment without bumping into each other?
2. Introduce children to stop and go signals (chapter 4).
Q. Do children stop when signal is sounded?
3. Introduce locomotor skills of walking, marching, galloping, and hopping (chapter 4).
Q. Are children swinging arms in opposition when walking and marching, are they leading with one foot when galloping, are they holding their arms out when hopping, and staying on balance and not falling?

Manipulative Activities (10 minutes)

4. Use beanbag activities to identify body parts (chapter 5).
Q. Do children know the different parts of their bodies and can they balance beanbags on the different parts? Does anyone need any help?
5. Introduce throwing and catching skills using punchball balloons (chapter 10).
Q. Can children toss balloons straight into the air? Are they tracking the balloons? Do children place their arms out in front of their bodies to prepare for catching the balloons?
6. Introduce striking with body parts using punchball balloons (chapter 11).
Q. Are children keeping a flat body part when striking?

Nonmanipulative Activities (7 minutes)

7. Introduce jumping from two-foot takeoff and two-foot landing using hoops and boxes (chapters 6 and 9).
Q. Do children concentrate on swinging arms when jumping?

Rhythm/Body Awareness Activity (3 minutes)

8. End class with body part identification song "My Head, My Shoulders, My Knees, My Toes" (chapter 5).

Q. Can children move in time with the music and touch appropriate body parts?

Review lesson activities with the children.

Lesson 2

Time: 30 minutes

Equipment: Stop and go signals, jump ropes, beanbags, punchball balloons, hoops, jump boxes, wedges or mats, and music ("My Head, My Shoulders, My Knees, My Toes")

In this lesson children review previously introduced skills of jumping, walking, galloping, hopping, identifying body parts, and striking with body parts.

In this lesson children learn pathway and directional concepts; how to swing rope when jumping rope; how to do a log roll (emphasizing all body parts moving together); how to do log rolls and jumps in an obstacle course sequence.

Travel Maps: Locomotor, jumping, body awareness, throwing, catching, striking with body parts, rolling

Locomotor Activities (10 minutes)

1. Review concepts of general and self-space and establish the movement environment (chapter 4).
Q. Can children recite the definitions of general and self-space?
2. Review stop and go signals (chapter 4).
Q. Are children stopping to listen when stop signal is sounded?
3. Review locomotor skills of walking, marching, galloping, and hopping (chapter 4).
Q. Can children perform the locomotor skills without bumping into classmates? Are they using all the general space without getting too close together?
4. Introduce concepts of pathways (zigzag, curved, and straight) and directions (forward, backward, and sideways) (chapter 4).
Q. Can children perform locomotor skills while moving in various pathways and directions?
5. Introduce jumping rope (chapter 5).
Q. Can all children find a place to jump away from classmates? Can children swing the rope over their heads without tangling it in their feet or around their heads?

Manipulative Activities (8 minutes)

6. Review body part identification activities using beanbags (chapter 5).
Q. Do all children know the parts of the body? (Any child who doesn't may need extra help.)
7. Review striking with body parts using punchball balloons (chapter 11).
Q. Can all children get their balloons and find a place to work? Are children keeping a flat body part when striking?
8. Review catching using punchball balloons (chapter 10).
Q. Are children placing their arms out in front of the body as they attempt to catch?

Nonmanipulative Activities (10 minutes)

9. Review jumping skills of two-foot takeoff and two-foot landing using hoops and boxes (chapters 6 and 9).
Q. Are children jumping from two feet and landing on two feet? (Give extra attention to children having difficulty.)
10. Introduce log roll (chapter 7).
Q. Can children move their legs at the same speed as their arms and roll straight?
11. Incorporate jumping and log roll activity into obstacle course sequence (chapter 9).
Q. Do children understand where to move in obstacle sequence? Teachers should help one child at a time do log rolls, while other children move around the room independently, jumping through a sequence of hoops and boxes.

Rhythms/Body Awareness Activity (2 minutes)

12. End class with body part identification song "My Head, My Shoulders, My Knees, My Toes" (chapter 5).
Q. Can children stay in time with the music and touch body parts when music suggests? (Some children will need help remembering which body part comes next in sequence.)

Review lesson activities with the children.

Lesson 3

Time: 30 minutes

Equipment: Rhythm sticks, music, Ethafoam pins or 2-liter soda bottles, jump ropes, balloons, paddles, beanbags, targets, mats and wedges, hoops, and boxes

In this lesson children review locomotor skills, direction and pathway concepts, jumping rope, log rolls, body part identification song.

In this lesson children learn to move around obstacles while performing locomotor skills; move rhythm sticks to beat of music; throw overhand while stepping with opposite foot; contact balloon with flat paddle; tuck the chin when doing a forward roll.

Travel Maps: Rhythm, locomotor, jumping, throwing, catching, striking with body parts, striking with paddles, rolling

Rhythms (5 minutes)

1. Introduce manipulative skills using rhythm sticks and choose appropriate song for the age group (chapter 15).
Q. Can children get out and put away the rhythm sticks in a safe way? Are children spaced far enough apart that they will not accidentally strike a classmate? Can children strike sticks at the appropriate time to the beat of the music?

Locomotor Activities (10 minutes)

2. Review locomotor activities using obstacles for children to move around (chapter 4). Review concepts of general and self-space and establish the movement environment along with stop and go signals (chapter 4). Review locomotor skills of walking, marching, galloping, and hopping. Review concepts of pathways (zigzag, curved, and straight) and directions (forward, backward, and sideways) (chapter 4).
Q. Can children move through environment without knocking over obstacles or bumping into classmates?
3. Introduce skipping (chapter 4).
Q. Are you focusing on introducing skipping so that children know what it is? Are you stressing the step-hop movement on one foot and then on the other? (Do not stress perfection in skipping; it may take several years for children to develop the skill.)
4. Review the skill of jumping rope (chapter 6).
Q. Can children jump over the rope on two feet and land on two feet?

Manipulative Activities (9 minutes)

5. Review catching (chapter 10) and striking skills (chapter 11) using balloons. Use these activities as a warm-up to striking activities with the balloon.
Q. Are children working by themselves? Are children tracking the balloon with their eyes?
6. Introduce striking with a paddle using balloons and paddles (chapter 13).

Q. Are children keeping a flat paddle when striking the balloon straight into the air?

7. Introduce throwing overhand; use the beanbags, wooden stand-up targets, and wall target (chapter 10).

Q. Do children step on the opposite foot when throwing?

Nonmanipulative Activities (5 minutes)

8. Review log roll and jumping activities in obstacle course formation.

Q. Are children following the sequence?

9. Introduce forward roll into the obstacle sequence.

Q. Are children tucking their chins to their chests when doing the roll? (Focus on helping children individually while other children go through the obstacle course.)

Rhythms/Body Awareness Activity (1 minute)

10. End class with body part identification song "My Head, My Shoulders, My Knees, My Toes" (chapter 5).

Q. Do most children by now know this song? (Give extra attention to children who have not picked up the movements.)

Review lesson activities with the children.

Lesson 4

Time: 30 minutes

Equipment: Rhythm sticks, music, obstacles for locomotor activities, jump ropes, balloons, paddles, beanbags, targets, mats, wedges, hoops, crawl-through shapes, music for "Tony Chestnut"

In this lesson children review rhythm stick activities; moving through obstacles; jumping rope; keeping paddles flat when striking balloons; stepping with the opposite foot when throwing overhand; log roll; tucking chin on forward roll.

In this lesson children learn to step with the opposite foot when throwing underhand; move through obstacles without bumping or touching them; identify names for different shapes; jump alternating from one-foot to two-foot and back to one-foot pattern; tuck chin when doing a backward roll.

Travel Maps: Rhythm, body awareness, locomotor, jumping, throwing, striking with paddles, rolling

Rhythms (5 minutes)

1. Repeat manipulative skills using rhythm sticks and choose appropriate song for the age group (chapter 15).
Q. Do children keep time with the beat of the music?

Locomotor Activities (8 minutes)

2. Review concepts of general and self-space and establish the movement environment (chapter 4) using obstacles for children to move around. Review stop and go signals (chapter 4). Review locomotor skills of walking, marching, galloping, hopping, and skipping (chapter 4). Review concepts of pathways (zigzag, curved, and straight) and directions (forward, backward, and sideways) (chapter 4).
Q. Can children move through the environment without knocking over the obstacles or bumping into classmates? (This is a good opportunity for the teacher to work with children who need individual help.)
3. Introduce jumping (chapter 6).
Q. Are children able to jump off one foot and land on the other? Are children staying in the air as long as possible?
4. Review jumping rope (chapter 6).
Q. Can any children swing the jump rope over their heads and jump more than one time? (Those children could make good demonstrators for others having difficulties.)

Manipulative Activities (8 minutes)

5. Use balloon activities with paddles (chapter 13).
Q. Can children strike balloon with flat paddle more than four or five times in a row? (Work individually with those who cannot.)
6. Repeat overhand throwing using targets (chapter 10).
Q. Can children hit the target? (If not, work individually with those children. Allow children to move closer to the target if needed.)
7. Introduce underhand throw (chapter 10).
Q. Are children stepping with opposite foot as in the overhand throw?

Nonmanipulative Activities (7 minutes)

8.   Review jumping, forward roll, and log roll using obstacle course. Add backward roll (chapter 7) and directional arrows (chapter 9) to obstacle course. Change line jumping through hoops to hopscotch formation (chapter 6). Also add body awareness activities of crawling through tunnels (chapter 5).

Q.   Are children tucking their chins to their chests? (Children can move on their own through the obstacle course, but work individually in presenting the backward roll.)

9.   By this time, most children can perform the forward roll by themselves and will not need help. Ask children who need help to skip forward roll station until help is available.

Q.   Can children move through the tunnel and identify shapes without touching or bumping into them?

Rhythms/Body Awareness (2 minutes)

10.   End class with body part identification song "Tony Chestnut" (chapter 5).

Q.   Do children clearly understood which movements to use during various parts of the song?

Review lesson activities with the children.

Lesson 5

Time: 30 minutes

Equipment: Ribbon sticks, music, hoops, jump ropes, Frisbee, paddles, cones, plastic balls, balance beams, obstacle course (teachers choose the activities they want to include in this week's sequence from past lessons), music for "Tony Chestnut"

In this lesson children review jumping rope and leaping and nonmanipulative obstacle course activities to coincide with balance beam activities.

In this lesson children learn to move ribbons in the air to form zigzag, straight, and curved pathways; throw a Frisbee using an across-body motion; balance on body parts with a wide base of support; extend the arms to assist in walking the balance beam; strike a ball off a cone using a forehand motion; and emphasize hitting the ball in the middle of the paddle.

Travel Maps: Rhythm, body awareness, jumping, throwing, striking with paddles, balance, rolling

Rhythms (5 minutes)

1. Introduce ribbon stick activities and choose appropriate song for the age group (chapter 15).
Q. Have children found a place to work where they will not accidentally strike a classmate with the ribbon sticks?

Locomotor Activities (6 minutes)

2. Practice jumping rope (chapter 6).
Q. Are children having trouble coordinating swinging the rope and jumping?
3. Review leaping skills using hoops (chapter 6).
Q. Have children arranged the hoops so that when they leap they are not close to other children? (Locate several children who are leaping very high when they perform the task and ask them to demonstrate so others can see how the skill can be done.)

Manipulative Activities (9 minutes)

4. Introduce sidearm throwing (chapter 10).
Q. Do children step with the right foot if they throw with the right arm? (The stepping pattern for this throwing motion is different than the overhand or underhand throw.)
5. Introduce forehand striking using paddles, cones, and plastic balls (chapter 13).
Q. Are children striking the ball in the middle of the paddle?

Nonmanipulative Activities (9 minutes)

6. Introduce balancing on body parts, using hoops as boundaries within which children can balance (chapter 8).
Q. Are children using a wide base of support when balancing?

7. Introduce balance beam activities at low level (chapter 8) and add balance beams to existing obstacle course. Because teachers will want to help children work on the beams and because the backward roll requires the teacher to spot, take the backward roll out of the obstacle course when using the beams.

Q. Do children move slowly across the beams while holding the arms out to the side? (Have several children demonstrate how they would jump off the beams and land on two feet if they were to fall.)

Rhythms/Body Awareness (1 minute)

8. End class with body part identification song "Tony Chestnut" (chapter 5).

Q. Are children able to follow along, touching body parts when instructed to do so by the music?

Review lesson activities with the children.

Lesson 6

Time: 30 minutes

Equipment: Ribbon sticks, music, jump ropes, cones, plastic balls, paddles, launch boards, beanbags, balance beams, obstacle course (teachers select equipment to coincide with balance beam practice)

In this lesson children review creating pathways with ribbon sticks; jumping rope; forehand swing with a paddle; balancing with a wide base of support; walking on balance beams with extended arms; selected obstacle course activities; body part identification with music.

In this lesson children learn to strike a ball in the middle of the paddle using a backhand motion and catch a beanbag while keeping their eyes on it.

Travel Maps: Rhythm, jumping, striking with paddles, catching, balance, rolling, locomotor

---

Rhythms (5 minutes)

1. Repeat ribbon stick activities and choose appropriate song for age group (chapter 15).
Q. Can children create various pathways in the air with the ribbons?

Locomotor Activities (4 minutes)

2. Practice jumping rope (chapter 6).
Q. How many continuous jumps can be done by children who have developed a successful jumping pattern?

Manipulative Activities (12 minutes)

3. Practice forehand and backhand striking skills using paddles, cones, and plastic balls (chapter 13).
Q. Stress keeping the paddle perpendicular to the floor and striking the ball with the middle of the paddle.
4. Introduce catching using launch boards (chapter 10).
Q. Are children watching the beanbag as it travels through the air?

Nonmanipulative Activities (8 minutes)

5. Review balancing on body parts, using hoops as boundaries in which children can balance (chapter 8).
Q. Do children attempt to keep a wide base of support even when balancing on just a few body parts?
6. Review balance beam activities in obstacle course formation with other skills.
Q. Do children hold their arms out to the side when walking on the beams? Do children jump off or step off the beam when they lose their balance? (If they step off review how to jump off and land on two feet. Make sure children are following the correct sequence and that they are not skipping stations.)

Rhythms/Body Awareness (1 minute)

7.   End class with body part identification song "Tony Chestnut" (chapter 5).

Review lesson activities with the children.

Lesson 7

Time: 30 minutes

Equipment: Scarves, music for scarf activities, jump ropes, launch boards, beanbags, scoops, balloons, balance boards (teacher selects equipment needed for the obstacle course)

In this lesson children review jumping rope; jumping and landing on two feet; catching using launch boards (with the emphasis on visually tracking the beanbag); skills in obstacle course sequence.

In this lesson children learn to move scarves in various pathways to the beat of the music; catch a beanbag in a scoop (stressing visual tracking); place nonkicking foot beside the ball when kicking; contact the ball with the shoelaces when punting; extend arms when balancing on balance boards.

Travel Maps: Rhythm, jumping, catching, kicking and punting, balance, rolling, body awareness

Rhythms (5 minutes)

1. Introduce scarf activities and choose appropriate song for age group (chapter 15).
Q. Are children able to move the scarves in various pathways around the body?

Locomotor Activities (3 minutes)

2. Practice jumping rope (chapter 6).

Manipulative Activities (12 minutes)

3. Review catching skills with launch boards and add scoops (chapter 10).
Q. Do children stomp on the proper place on the end of the board? (Select students to demonstrate if needed.) Are children moving the scoop to be directly under the beanbag?
4. Introduce kicking and punting using the balloons (chapter 12).
Q. When kicking are children placing their nonkicking foot beside the ball? When punting are children contacting the balloon with the top of the foot or the "shoelaces?"

Nonmanipulative Activities (8 minutes)

5. Introduce balance board activities (chapter 8).
Q. Are children using their extended arms to assist in balancing on the boards?
6. Review all skills in obstacle course sequence. As children have been working on this sequence concept for several weeks it may be time to allow them to create their own sequence. Experiment with asking the class to help decide which activities should be included in the day's obstacle course and in which sequence the equipment should be placed.

Rhythms (2 minutes)

7.   Select as a closing song a favorite that requires children to move to a musical beat.

Review lesson activities with the children.

Lesson 8

Time: 30 minutes

Equipment: Scarves, music to use with scarves, jump ropes, playground balls, Ethafoam hockey sticks and balloons, balance boards, equipment for obstacle course

In this lesson children review jumping rope; scarf activities (stressing moving in time to music and creating pathways); balance board activities (stressing extended arms); selected obstacle course skills.

In this lesson children learn to dribble a ball using the fingerpads; hold a hockey stick correctly; and strike a balloon with a full range of arm motion.

Note: In this lesson the teacher focus section is blank so teachers can practice writing their own focus before developing lesson plans.

Travel Maps: Rhythm, jumping, striking with body parts, striking with long-handled implements, balance, rolling

Rhythms (5 minutes)

1. Repeat scarf activities and choose appropriate song for age group (chapter 15).

Locomotor Activities (3 minutes)

2. Practice jumping rope (chapter 6).

Manipulative Activities (12 minutes)

3. Introduce dribbling (chapter 11).
4. Introduce using long-handled implements (chapter 14).

Nonmanipulative Activities (8 minutes)

5. Review balance skills using balance boards (chapter 8).
6. Review all skills in obstacle course sequence.

Rhythms (2 minutes)

7. Select a favorite closing song that requires children to move to a musical beat.

Review lesson activities with the children.

Appendix A

List of Selected Equipment Suppliers

This list includes prominent physical education equipment companies. It is only a starter list to help those unfamiliar with equipment sources. Inclusion on this list is not an endorsement.

BSN/GSC Corp.
P.O. Box 7726
Dallas, TX 75209

Childcraft Education Corp.
20 Kilmer Rd.
P.O. Box 3081
Edison, NJ 08818-3081

Chime Time
934 Anderson Dr.
Homer, NY 13077

Constructive Playthings
1227 E. 119th St.
Grandview, MO 64030

Flaghouse, Inc.
150 N. Macquesten Parkway
Mount Vernon, NY 10550

GameTime, Inc.
191 Kingsberry Rd.
Fort Payne, AL 35967

Gerstung/Gym-Thing, Inc.
6308 Blair Hill Ln.
Baltimore, MD 21209

Gibson, Inc.
P.O. Box 1444
Englewood, CO 80150

Gopher Sports Equipment
220 24th Ave. NW
Owatonna, MN 55060

Gym Closet
2511 Leach Rd.
Rochester Hills, MI 48309

J.L. Hammett Co.
Hammett Place, Box 545
Braintree, MA 02184

Kimbo
P.O. Box 477
Long Branch, NJ 07740

Lakeshore Curriculum Material Co.
2695 E. Pomingues St.
P.O. Box 6261
Carson, CA 90749

Mancino Manufacturing Co.
4962 Baynton St.
Philadelphia, PA 19144

McKinney Video Productions, Inc.
613 Silver Circle
Dalton, GA 30720
(Distributes a series of five video tapes that helps visually explain activities in this book.)

Ohio Art Co.
P.O. Box 111
Bryan, OH 43506

Snitz Manufacturing Co.
Box 76
East Troy, WI 53120

Sportime
2905 E. Amwiler Rd.
Atlanta, GA 30360

USC, Inc.
One Olympic Dr.
Orangeburg, NY 10962

Developmentally Appropriate Physical Education for Children*

As we enter the 21st century the importance and value of regular physical activity has been recognized as never before. Accompanying this recognition is the awareness that childhood is the time to begin the development of active and healthy lifestyles.

Children do not automatically develop the skills, knowledge, attitudes, and behaviors that lead to regular and enjoyable participation in physical activity. They must be taught. The responsibility for this instruction is vested primarily in physical education programs in the schools.

In recent years a growing body of research, theory, and practical experience has sharpened our understanding about the beneficial aspects of physical education programs for children—and those that are counterproductive. The purpose of this document is to describe, in a very straightforward way, practices that are both appropriate and inappropriate for children in preschool and elementary school physical education programs.

Quality Physical Education for Children

The Council on Physical Education for Children (COPEC), the nation's largest professional association of children's physical education teachers, believes that quality, daily physical education should be available to all children. Quality physical education is developmentally appropriate for children.

"Developmentally appropriate programs are both age appropriate and individually appropriate; that is, the program is designed for the age group served and implemented with attention to the needs and differences of the individual children enrolled" (NAEYC, 1986). The outcome of a developmentally appropriate program of physical education is an individual who is "physically educated."

In 1990, the National Association for Sport and Physical Education (NASPE) defined a physically educated person as one who:

- HAS learned the skills necessary to perform a variety of physical activities
- DOES participate regularly in physical activity
- IS physically fit
- KNOWS the implications of and the benefits from involvement in physical activities
- VALUES physical activity and its contributions to a healthful lifestyle

Developmentally appropriate physical education programs for children provide an important first step towards becoming a physically educated person.

Premises of Physical Education Programs for Children

In any discussion of physical education programs for children there are three major premises that need to be understood.

1. Physical education and athletic programs have different purposes.

---

*Reprinted by permission of the publisher, National Association for the Education of Young Children, Washington, D.C.

Athletic programs are essentially designed for youngsters who are eager to specialize in one or more sports and refine their talents in order to compete with others of similar interests and abilities. Developmentally appropriate physical education programs, in contrast, are designed for every child—from the physically gifted to the physically challenged. The intent is to provide children of all abilities and interests with a foundation of movement experiences that will eventually lead to active and healthy lifestyles—athletic competition may be one part of this lifestyle, but is not the only part.

2.   Children are not miniature adults.

Children have very different abilities, needs, and interests than adults. It is inadequate to simply "water down" adult sport or activity programs and assume that they will be beneficial. Children need, and learn from, programs that are designed specifically with their needs and differences in mind.

3.   Children in school today will not be adults in today's world.

More than ever before we are in a time of rapid change. Consequently, educators have the challenge of preparing children to live as adults in a world that has yet to be clearly defined and understood. The only certainty is that they will have different opportunities and interests than currently exist. Contemporary programs introduce children to the world of today, while also preparing them to live in the uncertain world of tomorrow. In brief, they help them learn how to learn—and to enjoy the process of discovering and exploring new and different challenges in the physical domain.

Tomorrow's physical activities may look quite different from today's. Present programs need to prepare children with basic movement skills that can be used in any activity, whether it be popular today or one yet to be invented. Mastery of basic skills encourages the development and refinement of more complex skills leading to the ultimate enjoyment of physical activity for its own sake.

Intended Audience

This document is written for teachers, parents, school administrators, policy makers, and other individuals who are responsible for the physical education of children. It is intended to provide specific guidelines that will help them recognize practices that are in the best interests of children (developmentally appropriate) and those that are counterproductive, or even harmful (developmentally inappropriate). It needs to be understood that the components described in this appendix are, in actuality, interrelated. They are separated here only for purposes of clarity and ease of reading. It should also be understood that these components are not all-inclusive. They do represent, however, most of the characteristics of developmentally appropriate programs of physical education for children.

Appropriate and Inappropriate Physical Education Practices

Component: Curriculum

Appropriate Practice

- The physical education curriculum has an obvious scope and sequence based on goals and objectives that are beneficial for all children. It includes a balance of skills, concepts, games, educational gymnastics, rhythms, and dance experiences designed to enhance the cognitive, motor, affective, and physical fitness development of every child.

Inappropriate Practice

- The physical education curriculum lacks developed goals and objectives and is based primarily upon the teacher's interests, preferences, and background rather than those of the children. For example, the curriculum consists primarily of large group games.

plored and recognized by instructors.
- Children do not receive opportunities to integrate their physical education experience with art, music, and other classroom experiences.

Component: Development of Movement Concepts and Motor Skills

Appropriate Practice

- Children are provided with plenty of worthwhile practice opportunities which enable them to develop a functional understanding of movement concepts (body awareness, space awareness, effort, and relationships) and build competence and confidence in their ability to perform a variety of motor skills (locomotor, non-locomotor, and manipulative).

Inappropriate Practice

- Children participate in a limited number of games and activities where the opportunity for individual children to develop basic concepts and motor skills is restricted.

Component: Cognitive Development

Appropriate Practice

- Physical education activities are designed with both the physical and the cognitive development of children in mind.
- Experiences which encourage children to question, integrate, analyze, communicate, and apply cognitive concepts, as well as gain a multi-cultural view of the world are provided, thus making physical education a part of the total educational experience.

Inappropriate Practice

- The unique role of physical education, which allows children to learn to move while also moving to learn, is not ex-

Component: Affective Development

Appropriate Practice

- Teachers intentionally design and teach activities throughout the year which allow children the opportunity to work together for the purpose of improving their social and cooperation skills. These activities also help children develop a positive self-concept.
- Teachers help children experience and feel the satisfaction and joy which results from regular participation in physical activity.

Inappropriate Practice

- Teachers fail to intentionally enhance the affective development of children when activities are excluded which foster the development of cooperation and social skills.
- Teachers ignore opportunities to help children understand the emotions they feel as a result of participation in physical activity.

Component: Concepts of Fitness

Appropriate Practice

- Children participate in activities that are designed to help them understand and value the important concepts of physical fitness and the contribution they make to a healthy lifestyle.

Inappropriate Practice

- Children are required to participate in fitness activities, but are not helped to understand the reasons why.

Component: Physical Fitness Tests

Appropriate Practice

- Physical fitness tests are used as part of the ongoing process of helping children understand, enjoy, improve, and/or maintain their physical health and well-being.
- Test results are shared privately with children and their parents as a tool for developing their physical fitness knowledge, understanding, and competence.
- As part of an ongoing program of physical education, children are physically prepared so they can safely complete each component of a physical test battery.

Inappropriate Practice

- Physical fitness tests are given once or twice a year solely for the purpose of qualifying children for awards or because they are required by a school district or state department.
- Children are required to complete a physical fitness test battery without understanding why they are performing the tests or the implications of their individual results as they apply to their future health and well-being.
- Children are required to take physical fitness tests without adequate conditioning (e.g., students are made to run a mile after "practicing" it only one day the week before).

Component: Calisthenics

Appropriate Practice

- Appropriate exercises are taught for the specific purpose of improving the skill, coordination, and/or fitness levels of children.
- Children are taught exercises that keep the body in proper alignment, thereby allowing the muscles to lengthen without placing stress and strain on the surrounding joints, ligaments, and tendons (e.g., the sitting toe touch).

Inappropriate Practice

- Children perform standardized calisthenics with no specific purpose in mind (e.g., jumping jacks, windmills, toe touches).
- Exercises are taught which compromise body alignment and place unnecessary stress on the joints and muscles (e.g., deep-knee bends, ballistic [bouncing] stretches, and standing straight-legged toe touches).

Component: Fitness as Punishment

Appropriate Practice

- Fitness activities are used to help children increase their physical fitness levels in a supportive, motivating, and progressive manner, thereby promoting positive lifetime fitness attitudes.

Inappropriate Practice

- Physical fitness activities are used by teachers as punishment for children's misbehavior (e.g., students running laps, or doing push-ups, because they are off-task or slow to respond to teacher instruction).

Component: Assessment

Appropriate Practice

- Teacher decisions are based primarily on ongoing assessments of children as they participate in physical education class activities (formative evaluation), and not on the basis of a single test score (summative evaluation).
- Assessment of children's physical progress and achievement is used to individualize instruction, plan yearly curriculum and weekly lessons, identify children with special needs, communicate with parents, and evaluate the program's effectiveness.

Inappropriate Practice

- Children are evaluated on the basis of fitness test scores or on a single physical skill test. For example, children receive a grade in physical education based on their scores on a standardized fitness test or on the number of times they can continuously jump rope.

Component: Regular Involvement for Every Child

Appropriate Practice

- Children participate in their regularly scheduled physical education class because it is recognized as an important part of their overall education.

Inappropriate Practice

- Children are removed from physical education classes to participate in classroom activities and/or as a punishment for not completing assignments, or for misbehavior in the classroom.

Component: Active Participation for Every Child

Appropriate Practice

- *All* children are involved in activities which allow them to remain continuously active.
- Classes are designed to meet a child's need for active participation in all learning experiences.

Inappropriate Practice

- Activity time is limited because children are waiting in lines for a turn in relay races, to be chosen for a team, or due to limited equipment or playing games such as Duck, Duck, Goose.
- Children are organized into large groups where getting a turn is based on individual competitiveness or aggressive behavior.
- Children are eliminated with no chance to re-enter the activity, or they must sit for long periods of time. For example, activities such as musical chairs, dodgeball, and elimination tag provide limited opportunities for many children, especially the slower, less agile ones who actually need activity the most.

Component: Dance/Rhythmical Experiences

Appropriate Practice

- The physical education curriculum includes a variety of rhythmical, expressive, and dance experiences designed with the physical, cultural, emotional, and social abilities of the children in mind.

Inappropriate Practice

- The physical education curriculum includes no rhythmical, expressive, or cultural dance experiences for children.
- Folk and square dances (designed for adults) are taught too early or to the exclusion of other dance forms in the curriculum or are not modified to meet the developmental needs of the children.

Component: Educational Gymnastics

Appropriate Practice

- Children are encouraged to develop skills appropriate to their ability and confidence levels in non-competitive situations centering around the broad skill areas of balancing, rolling, jumping and landing, and weight transfer.
- Children are able to practice on apparatus designed for their confidence and skill level, and can design sequences which allow for success at their personal skill level.

Inappropriate Practice

- All students are expected to perform pre-determined stunts and routines on and off apparatus, regardless of their skill level, body composition, and level of confidence.

- Routines are competitive, are the sole basis for a grade, and/or must be performed solo while the remainder of the class sits and watches.

Component: Games

Appropriate Practice

- Games are selected, designed, sequenced, and modified by teachers and/or children to maximize the learning and enjoyment of children.

Inappropriate Practice

- Games are taught with no obvious purpose or goal, other than to keep children "busy, happy, and good."

Component: Rules Governing Game Play

Appropriate Practice

- Teachers and/or children modify official rules, regulations, equipment, and playing space of adult sports to match the varying abilities of the children.

Inappropriate Practice

- Official, adult rules of team sports govern the activities in physical education classes, resulting in low rates of success and lack of enjoyment for many children.

Component: Forming Teams

Appropriate Practice

- Teams are formed in ways that preserve the dignity and self-respect of every child. For example, a teacher privately forms teams by using knowledge of children's skill abilities or the children form teams cooperatively or randomly.

Inappropriate Practice

- Teams are formed by "captains" publicly selecting one child at a time, thereby exposing the lower-skilled children to peer ridicule.
- Teams are formed by pitting "boys against the girls," thereby emphasizing gender differences rather than cooperation and working together.

Component: Gender-Directed Activities

Appropriate Practice

- Girls and boys are provided equal access to participation in individual, partner, small group, and team activities. Both girls and boys are equally encouraged, supported, and socialized towards successful achievement in all realms of physical activities.
- Statements by physical education teachers support leadership opportunities and provide positive reinforcement in a variety of activities which may be considered gender-neutral.

Inappropriate Practice

- Girls are encouraged to participate in activities which stress traditionally feminine roles, whereas boys are encouraged to participate in more aggressive activities.
- Boys are more often provided with leadership roles in physical education class. Statements by physical education teachers reinforce traditional socialization patterns which provide for greater and more aggressive participation by boys and lesser and more passive participation by girls.

Component: Number of Children on a Team

Appropriate Practice

- Children participate in team games (e.g., 2-3 per team), which allow for numerous practice opportunities while also allowing them to learn about the various aspects of the game being taught.

Inappropriate Practice

- Children participate in full sided games (e.g., the class of 30 is split into two teams of 15 and these two teams play each other) thereby leading to few practice opportunities.

Component: Competition

Appropriate Practice

- Activities emphasize self-improvement, participation, and cooperation instead of winning and losing.
- Teachers are aware of the nature of competition and do not *require* higher levels of competition from children before they are ready. For example, children are allowed to choose between a game in which score is kept and one that is just for practice.

Inappropriate Practice

- Children are *required* to participate in activities that label children as "winners" and "losers."
- Children are *required* to participate in activities that compare one child's or team's performance against others (e.g., a race in which the winning child or team is clearly identified).

Component: Success Rate

Appropriate Practice

- Children are given the opportunity to practice skills at high rates of success adjusted for their individual skill levels.

Inappropriate Practice

- Children are asked to perform activities which are too easy or too hard, causing frustration, boredom, and/or misbehavior.

- All children are expected to perform to the same standards without allowing for individual abilities and interests.

Component: Class Size

Appropriate Practice

- Physical education classes contain the same number of children as the classrooms (e.g., 25 children per class).

Inappropriate Practice

- Children participate in a physical education class which includes more children than the classroom. (For example, two or more classrooms are placed with one certified teacher and one or more teacher aides.)

Component: Days per Week/Length of Class Time

Appropriate Practice

- Children are given the opportunity to participate daily in scheduled, instructional physical education throughout the year, exclusive of recess.
- Length of class is appropriate for the developmental level of the children.

Inappropriate Practice

- Children do not receive daily, instructional physical education.
- Children's age and maturational levels are not taken into account when physical education schedules are developed.

Component: Facilities

Appropriate Practice

- Children are provided an environment in which they have adequate space to move freely and safely. Both inside and outside areas are provided so that classes need not be cancelled, or movement severely limited, because of inclement weather.

Inappropriate Practice

- Physical education classes are regularly held in a school hallway or in a classroom thereby restricting opportunities to move freely and without obstructions.

Component: Equipment

Appropriate Practice

- Enough equipment is available so that each child benefits from maximum participation. For example, every child in a class would have a ball.
- Equipment is matched to the size, confidence, and skill level of the children so that they are motivated to actively participate in physical education classes.

Inappropriate Practice

- An insufficient amount of equipment is available for the number of children in a class (e.g., one ball for every four children).
- Regulation or "adult size" equipment is used which may inhibit skill development, injure, or intimidate the children.

Component: PE and Recess

Appropriate Practice

- Physical education classes are planned and organized to provide children with opportunities to acquire the physical, emotional, cognitive, and social benefits of physical education.

Inappropriate Practice

- "Free-play," or recess, is used as a *substitute* for daily, organized physical education lessons. Free-play, in this case, is characterized by a lack of goals, organization, planning, and instruction.

Component: Field Days

Appropriate Practice

- The field day, if offered, is designed so that every child is a full participant and derives a feeling of satisfaction and joy from a festival of physical activity.
- Opportunities are provided for children to voluntarily choose from a variety of activities that are intended purely for enjoyment.

Inappropriate Practice

- Field days, if offered, are designed so that there is intense team, group, or individual competition with winners and losers clearly identified.
- One or two children are picked to represent an entire class, thereby reducing others to the role of spectator.

Sample Lesson Plan

In this lesson children will learn about_____

_____

_____

Length of class _____

Travel maps used _____

_____

Needed equipment_____

_____

Skill-Development Activities	Teacher Observation

Note: Lesson plan activities in chapter 16 are to be placed on the lesson plan form. Place activities that are numbered (1, 2, 3) under "skill-development activities." List observational questions shown with a letter (Q) under "teacher observation." Put information outside those two categories in appropriate place under equipment, length of class, travel maps used, or what children will learn. Place any other information not included in these groups on the lesson plan in the order listed.

References

Corbin, C. (1973). *A textbook of motor development.* Dubuque, IA: Brown.

Council on Physical Education for Children (1991). *Developmentally appropriate physical education for children—A position statement.* Unpublished committee work, National Association for Sport and Physical Education, Washington, DC.

Flinchum, B. (1975). *Motor development in early childhood.* St. Louis: Mosby.

Graham, G. (1987). Motor skill acquisition—An essential goal of physical education program. *Journal of Physical Education, Recreation and Dance,* **58**, 44-48.

Graham, G., Holt/Hale, S., & Parker, M. (1987). *Children moving: A teacher's guide to developing a successful physical education program.* Mountain View, CA: Mayfield.

Hammett, C.T. (1992). *Movement activities for early childhood.* Champaign, IL: Human Kinetics.

Pica, R. (1990). *Preschoolers moving and learning.* Champaign, IL: Human Kinetics.

Physical Education Outcomes Committee. (1990). *Physical Education Outcomes.* Unpublished committee work, National Association for Sport and Physical Education, Washington, DC.

Poest, C.A., Williams, J.R., Witt, D.D., & Atwood, M.E. (1990, July). Challenge me to move: Large muscle development in young children. *Young Children,* pp. 4-10.

Stillwell, J. (1987). *Making and using creative play equipment.* Champaign, IL: Human Kinetics.

Wickstrom, R. (1977). *Fundamental motor patterns.* Philadelphia: Lea & Febiger.

Zaichkowsky, L.D., Zaichkowsky, L.B., & Martinek, T. (1980). *Growth and development: the child and physical activity.* St. Louis: Mosby.

Index